SAINT CROSS

England's Oldest Almshouse

St Cross church, east end from the Park.

SAINT CROSS

England's Oldest Almshouse

Peter Hopewell

Phillimore

1995

Published by
PHILLIMORE & CO. LTD.
Shopwyke Manor Barn, Chichester, West Sussex

ISBN 0 85033 965 0

Printed in Great Britain by
BOOKCRAFT (BATH) LTD.
Midsomer Norton, Avon

Contents

List of Illustrations

Frontispiece: St Cross church

All photographs are by John Russell, Orion Photo Services, Bracknell, except that of the Rev. A.S. Outhwaite, which is by kind permission of the Hampshire County Chronicle.

Preface

As with anyone who writes a book such as this, I am grateful to a vast number of people for their help. Some have been mentioned under the title of bibliography, even though their valuable contribution was by word of mouth rather than written. I must also mention the splendid work done by Gill Rushton in setting out on the long task of cataloguing the many papers of St Cross. Most of all, I have to thank my wife, Daphne, for reading half-completed and completed sections of the script, and making many helpful suggestions. The improvements are hers, and the faults that remain are mine. Finally, I would thank Hon. Christopher Chetwode for his tremendous co-operation in this project, and all those at Phillimore who gave continuous and much appreciated help.

Foreword
by the Earl of Malmesbury

The Hospital of St Cross has had a long and important history. A Pope excommunicated a village for quarrelling with it. A King sent his troops to ensure that his choice of Master was installed. Archbishops chose it for their favourites. Bishops reserved the Mastership for their relatives. It was so wealthy in days gone by that some Masters were tempted to rob it. Others, however, worked selflessly for the benefit of the Brethren. It is this central core of protection for those living within the almshouse and the sense of security and peace, that is pre-eminent at St Cross. This feeling of calm and consideration in the face of troubled times, makes the history of St Cross even more fascinating than would otherwise be the case. I have great pleasure in commending this full history (the first since 1868) of the two foundations that make up the Hospital to all who are interested in local history and in St Cross in particular.

Malmesbury

CHAPTER *I*

Foundations

The Hospital of St Cross was founded in deeply troubled times for the nation. Henry I, in a very active life, had sired at least twenty-one children, but only two were legitimate. Of these two, the son and heir had been drowned in the tragic loss of the *White Ship*. As a result, the heir presumptive was Henry's daughter, Matilda. She was important enough to have been married to, and widowed by, the Holy Roman Emperor. Nevertheless, King Henry felt unsure of her position, and had persuaded all his nobles to swear allegiance to her, and to accept her as 'Queen to be', whilst he was still alive. Matilda was haughty and imperious. Her second marriage to Geoffrey of Anjou was unpopular with the barons and her position was weakened by the fact that there were obvious male claimants to the throne. Theobald and Stephen, the two sons of Henry's sister Adela, had strong support from the nobles, many of whom regarded them as having a better right to the crown than Matilda. Although Theobald was the elder, Stephen was the more active, and slipped across the Channel from France at Henry's death. He managed to persuade the people of London to 'elect' him King, at least saving England from having a monarch called Theobald. He quickly raced down to Winchester, the official capital of the country, to seize the Treasury. Here he at once gained the support of his powerful half-brother, the Bishop, Henry de Blois. As Stephen was known to be a brave warrior, but lacking in statesmanship and firmness, he was regarded by many barons as being a man they could manipulate. Disregarding their oaths, they deserted Matilda for him. Almost at once, the country fell into bitter civil war, which led to the next twenty years to be dubbed 'the Anarchy' by historians. The English Chronicle for 1137 reported: 'Then was corn dear, and flesh and cheese and butter, for there was none in the land; wretched men starved with hunger; some lived on alms that had been erstwhile rich; the earth bare no corn; one might as well have tilled the sea; men said openly that Christ and his saints slept.' It is into this background that the foundation of St Cross has to be placed.

Winchester was important ecclesiastically, and Henry de Blois, the Bishop of Winchester, both because of his office as Papal Legate and his royal connections, was a powerful man. During the civil war, he supported first Stephen, then Matilda, but finally Stephen. He was a grandson of William the Conqueror, nephew to Henry I, half-brother to Stephen and cousin to Matilda. As a young boy, perhaps not entirely to his choice, he had become a monk of the Cluniac order. At Cluny, he was taught the lesson of public charity, for which the order was famous. He did not, however, lose his pride and ambition.

1 *Henry de Blois, as shown on one of his seals.*

At the early age of 28, he was created Bishop of Winchester. Because of his background and his wealth, Henry de Blois felt that he really ought to be an archbishop. He set out on a policy to raise the diocese of Winchester into an archdiocese, embracing the seven western bishoprics. It was necessary, therefore, to do something connected with the Church to make his administrative area even more important than it already was. Henry was a very wealthy man, and he still remembered the Cluniac teaching of charity. He determined to found an almshouse of considerable size and importance, using, at first, his own resources. This would draw attention to him both as a man of compassion and of religion.

Just 'without the city walls', and a pleasant walk along the riverside from Winchester, lay the village of Sparkford. As its name implies, it was a place built around or near a ford marked by a dry tree or brushwood. The village had a degree of importance as it lay near the major east-west route across the country from Dover to around Weston-super-Mare. It was also the point at which a spur road used the ford to lead on down to Southampton. In days long gone, there seems to have been a religious establishment nearby—perhaps a monastery. Records suggest that, somewhere in that area, a building belonging to the church was destroyed in either 745, 842, 871, or 1001. Godwin, in his *De Praesulibus*, written in 1223, talking of de Blois as a leader, says: 'Now concerning the monuments of his bounty and liberality you shall understand that he founded that worthy Hospital of St. Cross near Winchester. In which place something had been built long before to some such good use, but it was destroyed by the Danes and quite ruinated till he reedified it or rather laid new foundations in the same place Anno 1132 and endowed it with the Revenue it now hath.' Any one of the dates quoted might be correct, as there was a Danish assault on either Winchester, Southampton, or the general Wessex area at those times. At any rate, there was a church-owned, ruined building standing in a goodly area of ground in Sparkford.

There is a legend which prettily ties Henry de Blois and his charity to the area. It is said that the Bishop was walking in the water meadows —one of his favourite strolling places—when he met a milkmaid who was carrying a babe in her arms and a milkpail on her head. From a distance, Henry thought that he was seeing the Virgin Mary, wearing her typical tall crown and carrying the infant Jesus. When the milkmaid came close to him, she told him how Sparkford was suffering and how everyone was lacking food, and begged him to do something 'out of his charity' for the inhabitants. Impressed by his feeling that he had at first seen the Virgin Mary, he was swiftly convinced by the milkmaid that he had a duty to perform in Sparkford.

There was thus a linking of ambition, desire to perform a charitable deed, and the existence of a suitable Church-owned site. Henry was quite clear in his own mind who were to be the recipients of his charity. 'The manner of the service and constituents made by me are these: Thirteen poor men, feeble and so reduced in strength that they can scarcely or not at all support themselves without other aid, shall remain in the same Hospital constantly; to whom necessary clothing, provided by the Prior of the Establishment, shall be given, and beds fit for their infirmities; and a daily good loaf of wheaten bread of the weight of five measures, three dishes at dinner, and one for supper', which was to be a 'pittance as the day should require'. They were also to have 'drink of good stuff in sufficient quantity'. Most people drank beer, as the water was not trusted, but it was usually weak or 'small' beer. This was not to be considered adequate for the men of St Cross, who were specifically to receive the 'good stuff', or strong beer. As the 'sufficient quantity' of beer came to be defined as 'three quarts' each day, they must have been a merry crew! It is now generally accepted that five measures of bread is the equivalent of modern two and three quarter pounds. Note that here again the bread was to be a 'good loaf', not the rough ground stuff of the peasant and worker. Special names, mortrell and wastell, were given to some of the foods. Medievalists now agree that mortrell was a dish consisting of a mixture of milk and yolk of eggs, whilst wastell meant any type of roll of bread made of finer flour than was usual. Both sound nourishing for the elderly men. This is the detail given in the Hospital Constitution. The Harleian records quote the diet as five marks weight of wheaten bread, one and a half gallons of beer, a sufficiency of pottage, three dishes at dinner, one dish at supper, all to cost no more than three pence per day per person. (Throughout this book, the old notations for coins have been used. Thus £ s. d. means pounds, shillings and pence. £1 would still be written thus. There were 20 shillings to a pound, thus a shilling would be written now as 5p. Twelve pence made up a shilling, so theoretically each old 'd' should be written as 5/12p. This has led to considerable fancy division and approximation—6d. is 2.5p, 9d. is 3.75p, for example, which ignores the fact that there are no 0.5p's or 0.25p's. Thus a medieval £7 8s. 4d. would now be written as £7.42, which certainly makes no attempt to equate its modern day purchasing power.)

If any of the brethren recovered and became able to look after themselves (despite or because of the amount of ale supped?), they were to be 'dismissed with honour and sent out of' the Hospital to make room for a replacement brother who could not look after himself. Hospital, of course, is used in the early meaning of a place to stay, from which we may be said to derive hotel, rather than in its modern sense, despite the fact that it was to provide refuge for weak men. At this time, the number 13 was not regarded as being unlucky, but almost as one to be venerated, as it commemorated Jesus and his 12 apostles.

In addition to the 13 men living in the Hospital, de Blois also provided charity for 100 who lived out. 'Besides these thirteen poor men, one hundred poor and modest persons, of the most indigent that can be found, shall be received at the hour of dinner, to whom a coarser bread of the same weight shall be given, and two messes of flesh or fish, as shall seem meet, according to the convenience of the day, and a cup of the same measure, who, having left dinner, may be allowed to take away whatever of food or drink shall be left over.' The drink allowed to each man, defined in 'a cup of the same measure', was that three quarts allowed to the inmates. For the outliers, however, it was of small beer, so that while the quantity remained equal to that of the brethren, the quality was not quite as good. The meal was to be cooked by the 'Hundred-men-cooke', served from the 'Hundred-men-pot' using the 'Hundred-men-ladel'. Again, the Harleian records have other details and quote the menu as one loaf of barley bread, one dish of pulse, one salt fish, two eggs or a farthing's-worth of cheese, and three quarts of beer. For the distribution of this charity, a special 'The Hundred-menne-halle', close by the Hospital gate, was to be built. Giving alms to outsiders was not unique to St Cross, although there were only three or four others (notably in York and Norwich) which did so.

These constitutions make it clear that the founder was determined to be generous. Certainly, in times of hardship such as existed then, the provision was far beyond what the peasant and serf class might expect. With this in mind, the fact that the 100 men were allowed to take away what they did not eat or drink at table, becomes of considerable importance. It may be said to have represented the equivalent of a modern welfare system, providing the very basics of life for the poorest people of Winchester. It is hard to estimate the population of the city in the 1130s. The Domesday Survey, which completely omitted Winchester and London, worked out that there were 9,082 inhabitants of Hampshire. Probably Winchester itself then had about 5,000 people living in it. Professor Postan in 1966 suggested a figure of about 7,500 in the 1130s. National population movements and natural increase would seem to support this figure, if we accept 5,000 in William I's time. Postan also suggests that the average family in England consisted then of 4.5, including children. If we accept this figure, and its wonderful provision of a half human somewhere in each household, then there would be about 1,660 families in Winchester. Of these, 100 could receive bread and the remains of a meal brought home in a 'doggy bag' via de Blois' hundred-men's Charity. We can thus deduce that apparently about six to seven per cent of Winchester's population received aid from St Cross. As there was usually a royal house-hold, a strong merchant class, plus a powerful Church representation living in the city, none of which needed charity, it does seem that a large portion of the urban poor was helped by the Hospital of St Cross. Certainly, from the very fact of 100 being helped, the Charity did not just cater for those living in Sparkford. Moreover, in a time when everyone was used to walking, it was not far from the city centre, either by the meadows or the main road—perhaps no more than half an hour away at the most.

Henry de Blois could not forget his Cluniac training or the fact that he was a bishop. He talks of the Hospital as the one 'I, for the health of the souls of myself, my predecessors, and the kings of England have newly instituted without the walls of Winchester'. He was attempting to 'buy' salvation for himself and others by his own good works. The benefi-ciaries were to be 'the poor of Christ, meekly and devoutly serving God'. There were to be regular daily services held in the chapel built for the brethren. It is sometimes said that the church, when it was eventually finished, was too big for 13 poor men, and from this has come the deduction that the hundred poor were also expected to worship there. This is almost certainly inaccurate. To maintain the religious side of his foundation, de Blois provided for a Master, a Steward, four chaplains, 13 clerks and seven choristers. In addition, there were four servers, two servants, three bakers, three brewers, one cook, one man maintaining the grounds, two grooms, and three cart drivers. There was thus an establishment of 45 to look after the religious and temporal needs of the 13 men of the original foundation—generous provision by any standards. These people were all expected to worship in the chapel, virtually ordered to do so by Henry de Blois. Remembering that seats were not provided, that there were several altars, and that the building progressed but slowly, it is easy to see that the 58 inmates who were bidden to worship could well use a fairly large chapel without calling on the hundred poor, who were not so bidden. Later, 13 poor scholars of the school of St Swithun were added to the list of those to be fed free at St Cross. These scholars were the lineal descendants of the pupils at the grammar school, set up, it is claimed, as part of the Old Minster foundation in 648. Their diet was apparently the same as that given to the hundred poor, so they, too, were probably able to feed their families from St Cross. Certainly they were expected to worship in the church. It is possible that the pupils represent the existence of a small school within the precincts of St Cross, perhaps on the grass in the open air. The continuity of education in the area may thus be seen to have depended upon the Hospital.

One of the great Cluniac traditions was that of providing sustenance for travellers, when roads were poor and towns and villages widely scattered. St Cross accepted this duty, along with the task of looking after the poor. At first, the amount given was a bottle of wine holding about two and a half pints and a loaf of bread to each wayfarer. Perhaps this helps to explain the winding path of some roads. The Wayfarers' Dole is still available at St Cross, maintaining a tradition of over eight hundred and fifty years—but now it has been reduced to a small metal goblet of ale and a tiny cube of bread. The bread was produced until the 1970s in the bakery said to be on the site of the original bakery of Sparkford.

There was a yet more general call to charity, lest the founder had omitted anything or anybody: 'And other benefits also, to be mercifully performed to those in need, we command to be done according to the ability of the House'. Certainly, the whole idea was one which would have commended itself to a Beveridge of modern times.

As a cleric, however unwillingly at first, and however hard he tried to keep a foot firmly in the lay camp by building castles, Henry de Blois would naturally look at his charity from a Church point of view. 'All these things have I appointed to be observed in the aforesaid House of God, for ever to be continued and faithfully preserved by you, but preserving in all things the canonical justice of the Bishop of Winchester, that the appointment and admission of the said prior of the said hospital may be in the hands of the said bishop. And that the rents, together with all the appurtenances, bestowed upon the hospital by me, may remain, without disturbance or misapplication, for the purpose of the said hospital.' It is clear that Henry was setting up a charity with a close connection to the Church. Even its head was called a prior, though he rapidly became known as Master. Any inmate was a brother, though he took no vows and definitely belonged to no monastic order. Thus, although there was a close link to the Church, this was to be no monastery, nor could it be regarded as anything but a lay establishment of charity

2   *Receiving the Wayfarers' Dole in the Second World War.*

whose administration was in the hands of clerics. At this stage, there was no stated need for the Master to be a clergyman, and certainly, if he were, he would be one without cure of souls. Perhaps there was no need to state the qualification of being a priest, as few others had the education to carry out the job, and the bishop was going to appoint him anyhow.

(All these charters were in Latin, and I have deliberately throughout used semi-archaic translations in order, I hope, to give the flavour of age to what is written. Thus *'Ita viribus attenuati ut vix aut numquam sine alterius adminiculo se valeant sustenare'* becomes 'so reduced in strength that they can scarcely or not at all support themselves without other aid', although I know that modernists would produce a shorter and snappier phrase.)

Building St Cross was a very long-drawn-out affair. The early stages are not at all clearly defined. In the dry conditions of the 1980s, looking down at the site from the air revealed foundation lines of cell-like structures in the field to the south of the church. Perhaps these were the original rooms for the men of the Charity. Sparkford could not provide sufficient skilled men for such an undertaking. Masons were brought in from other areas. They built lodges against the first walls for their shelter—and even today, Freemasons and Trade Unions meet in lodges. Scattered around the church, there are almost forty different masons' marks. It is not clear whether these really have some cabalistic significance, as has been suggested, or are merely the marks of masons on the work they did—a sort of graffiti signature in stone or a sign that a particular mason was due for payment to that point. There are signs which resemble spiders gone mad, the cross of St Cross, the paschal P, sunbursts, an elementary *fleur de lys*, what looks like a star of David, an arrow, two crosses as if from a start on noughts and crosses, a simple plus, an F, and even a backwards J.

Most of us have sung the Victorian nursery rhyme *See-saw Margery Daw*. Although revived in comparatively modern times, the rhyme had its origins in de Blois' recruiting call. It was no good posting a notice asking for workers to report to the site, as they could not read. Instead, the vacancies had to be called. 'See Saw' enacts the sound of saws at work, for carpenters were needed. To Hampshire men, Henry de Blois became Anglicised as Messer dee Blaw—Margery Daw. Johnny was the name for any worker. If he went to work for the bishop, he 'shall have a new master'. The wage was colossal—a penny a day, though he won't have to work any faster. This would certainly be a great attraction, for it was well beyond anything that might be earned by a free agricultural worker. By comparison, the modern version is pouring scorn on the lowly wage, a penny a day, available. The similarities and differences between old and new are easily seen when reading the whole of each one.

Original: See Saw, Messer de Blaw,
Johnny shall have a new Master.
He shall get a penny a day,
Yet he shan't have to work any faster.

Modern: See Saw, Margery Daw,
Johnny shall have a new master,
He shall get but a penny a day,
'Cos he can't work any faster.

3 *King Stephen's table.*

The link between old and new is made even firmer by Mee, as he writes that the oval table with a Purbeck marble top now in the Brethren's Hall is the one on which 'Bishop Blois would pay his hundred masons a penny a day'. It is said that it was actually made for King Stephen, as a present from de Blois, to persuade the King to forget his support of Matilda. Later it was brought from Winchester Castle to St Cross. Age-wise, this is a possibility, as the top appears to be 12th-century, although the oval shape is not usually found until the 1600s. Perhaps a larger circular table was reshaped for some reason at that later date. De Blois did introduce the use of Purbeck rather than Caen marble into buildings such as the Cathedral.

Little still exists of the earliest work at St Cross. Oldest is the south sacristy. Built without a keystone, it has vaulted ribs, with the same demi-roll and two half-hollows that are to be found in work done in Winchester Cathedral in 1107. Dating the first buildings and foundation of St Cross is not easy. People did not set a neat foundation stone in the wall, with careful notes as to what distinguished person had carried out the ceremony of laying the stone. Instead, the first labourer came and cut the first turf, and the first mason laid the first stone, and work just went ahead.

One part of the earliest building is the 'triple door' in the south-east wall, which is now closed up. It seems to have been where an outside cloister led into the church, and had to be twisted to one side in order to avoid a buttress. Indeed, it is even possible that the sacristy may itself have originally been part of a cloister which may perhaps have led

4 *The triple arch.*

from the brothers' quarters to the south and into the church. From an architectural historian's point of view, the church is interesting as an example of transition from one style to another. This triple door or arch is widely argued about and there are many theories as to its real purpose.

In the choir, there are Purbeck marble bases to the two piers there. These are said by Crook to be the earliest examples of the use of this stone in a major weight-bearing load. English craftsmen could not handle this material. It is thus reasonable to suppose that the marble carvers from Tournai, at work in the Cathedral, also operated in St Cross. The link between de Blois, Cathedral and Hospital makes this likely.

The old documents of the Hospital give another hint as to a possible foundation date. The first Master is named and confirmed in March 1137 in a papal bull as Robert of

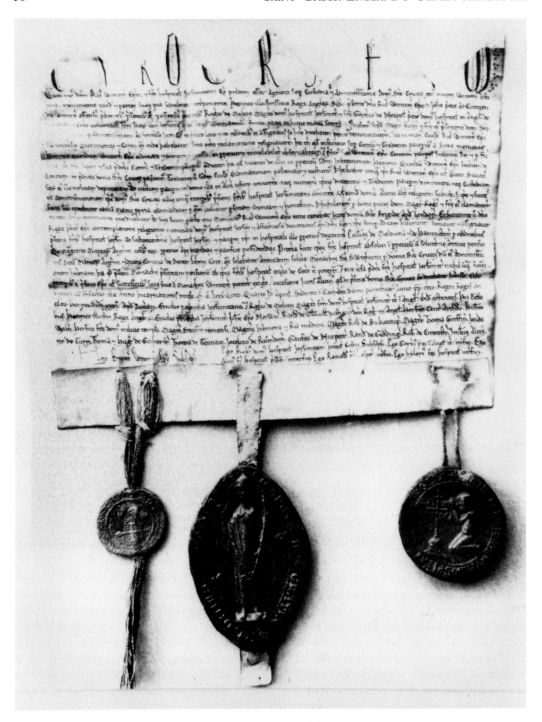

5   *Papal bull, confirming Robert of Limesia as Master.*

Limesia. The date of his institution is not given, though he was clearly in office before that date. It has been suggested that he was, in fact, a monk from Limes (hence Limesia) on what is now the Franco-Belgian border. This would fall in readily with the usage of the times, for all the best plums fell into the laps of the French or men of French origin. Ecclesiastically, it is known that a wave of French monks came over to England in the 1120s, so a date for the institution, close to the late 1120s, is reasonable. There is also a persistent story that Robert was a monk at Winchester. Apparently he made himself a nuisance in the then monastery by constantly arguing about matters. He was, therefore, promoted to St Cross in order to get him out of Henry's immediate proximity. He must still have been Master in 1153, though not after 1171, for he is found in a document dated as between 1153-1171, the second half of de Blois' ministry, as witness to a restoration of lands, including 'Burclere and Chiltecombe except Merdone Park', to the monks of St Swithun. These were properties which had belonged to the church at the time of Henry de Blois' consecration as bishop, but which he had taken into his own hand since.

Clearly, if the Pope were prepared to take notice of the new foundation, in a special bull in 1137, it is only reasonable to assume that some sort of building existed before that date. It was the custom in monastic settlements only to ask papal blessing when the monks actually had a place in which to pray and at least rudimentary living quarters. Whilst St Cross was not monastic, Henry's training was, and he could reasonably be expected to act from the instinct of his training. Robert would, therefore, have been commended to the Pope only when these basic requirements existed, and the foundation of the Charity would pre-date this. It would be many years before the impressive church began to be built to the north of the first simple dwellings and chapel, if only because it would have taken the founder some time to organise the necessary finance, rich man though he might be.

Obviously, Henry de Blois must have written to Pope Innocent II asking for the confirmation of his choice of Master of his new Charity before the Pope would need to consider the matter. Writing a letter in those days was not just a simple matter of a secretary swiftly taking dictation, transferring it to her word processor, putting it into a correctly addressed envelope, sticking a stamp on it, and posting it in the nearest post box, so that it could be received within a few days. Every word in Henry's time would have to be taken down in longhand, then transferred on to a parchment, in beautiful writing that would be appropriate for a letter to the Pope. Next it would be given to a messenger, who would carry it on horseback from St Cross to Southampton. There would then be the need to find a ship about to cross the Channel, always assuming that the wind was in the right quarter. Next came the long ride, on not particularly good roads, through France and over the Alps to Rome. Letter writing was not something that was entered into lightly and completed swiftly. It is certain that from the moment Henry wrote, the Pope considered his reply, wrote it, and returned it, some months must have elapsed. Thus, since the Pope's confirmation is dated March 1137, then the foundation of St Cross cannot possibly have been later than some time in 1136, though probably somewhat earlier. In 1157, de Blois, writing to Pope Adrian said: 'that I should make known to you by these present letters that in less than three years after my promotion I gave for the poor in Christ, houses and certain other benefits outside the walls of Winchester'. He became bishop in 1129, and this letter, therefore, the earliest to quote a date, and one quoted by the founder who might be expected to know, would put St Cross's foundation squarely at 1132. There is a window in the Master's Office, bearing the name of de Blois, the date 1129, and the word 'Fundator'. Presumably the date refers to Henry's elevation to the see of Winchester, but there is a vague chance that it alludes to the foundation of the charity, which is why it is in St Cross. It is thus just possible that the Hospital was founded in 1129, though it seems unlikely. The window also includes the arms of a 17th-century Master, Compton, and a bishop's mitre. During the great lawsuit of the 19th century, official documents accepted by the Attorney-General talk of the foundation having taken place 'about the year 1132' and list lands transferred to the Hospital by Henry de Blois at that time. This is also the date given by Godwin as previously quoted. In his book on schools in medieval England, A.F. Leach quotes a date of 1130 for the setting up of the Hospital and the provision for the education of poor scholars within its walls. The celebration of 850 years of life in 1986 is thus probably about four years too little, and 1132 is the most likely date of foundation.

CHAPTER II

Bishop takes Knight

There are a number of letters from successive Popes dealing with the business of St Cross in its early days. As the Pope was Head of Christendom, and Christendom embraced all the European nations, with one Pope feeling confident enough of his power to divide the world according to his line, he was clearly a man of immense influence. That he should write on St Cross' internal matters shows the great importance attached to the Hospital. Certainly, the times at which the letters were written show that the Charity was in the forefront of Papal politics. When Innocent II confirmed Robert as Master, he was involved in a war to assert his right to the Papacy. Indeed, his opponent, Anacletus, had been crowned Pope and it was only his death in 1138 and the stout support of St Bernard that saved Innocent. Lucius II had merely a one-year, troubled reign, being killed whilst storming the Capitol trying to drive his enemies out. Even so, in 1144, he confirmed the Charters and specifically ordered the tithes of Twyford and Fareham to be given to the Charity. Eugenius III struggled from his election in 1145 until 1152 to assert his authority over Rome, even using the weapon of starvation to force the city and Senate to submit. Yet in 1151 he found time to issue an instrument passing the Hospital into the control of the Knights of St John. Adrian IV, England's only Pope, continued the struggle with Rome, and placed the city under an Interdict to bring it to heel. At almost the same time, he confirmed all the arrangements Bishop Henry had made for his Charity. Alexander III had to face a challenger to the throne in Victor. Bit by bit, he won over the rulers of Europe to his side in a series of Councils starting at Pavia in 1160. He was thus involved in immense diplomatic activity across the continent. Yet he found time to write to 'the venerable, the Bishop of Winchester' (Henry was still living), approving the work of the Hospital 'after the steps of our predecessors of happy memory, Innocent, Lucius, Eugenius, and Adrian'. Even when times were difficult for the Popes on the European stage, they still found it worthwhile to think of and write about affairs in that little corner of Hampshire, St Cross. Their letters also show the high regard for the institution, in that in almost every case they put the Hospital under their personal protection and warn all clerics and other persons of the unpleasant results to them if they did not leave the place alone, and the spiritual rewards granted to those who helped it.

Henry de Blois was a rich man and finance was one of his strengths. As Abbot of Glastonbury, he had reorganised the Abbey's finances and made it one of the wealthiest in England. Much later, he returned to Cluny and rescued its finances. As an educated

6   *Window in Master's Office. Note words
calling Henry de Blois the Founder
(Fundator); script surrounded by Cardinal's
hat tassels. The date 1129 is in the dark
square below. The arms and bishop's mitre
above refer to Compton, a later Master and
Bishop of London.*

man, he had an interest in Greek and Roman sculptures. A contemporary report of 1151 credits him with having bought sculptures in Rome and then shipping them back to England—a very expensive business. Just as he was prepared to use his money on cultural aims, so he at first determined to finance his Charity from his very deep pocket. However, it was soon clear that the size of the buildings needed, and the very ambitious aims of the Charter, meant that money had to be found from other sources.

There is a splendid suggestion that he had to resort to money-lenders. In a land as disturbed as England, only people with Henry's connections were likely to have the right sort of credit ratings to expect loans. Certainly, Henry had those ratings! Apparently he was lent the money on the sole condition that if the money-lender fell on hard times, he would be given a place in St Cross. The civil war cost many people both lives and property. The money-lender failed, and he did, in fact, end his life as one of Henry's poor old men.

Bishop Henry had another well-filled coffer that he could raid. With the agreement and support of the Pope, he was able to pass a number of tithes to St Cross. The first list of churches quotes 'St Peter at Upham, the chapels of Durlia, Curia and Brixedona'. Brixedona is the modern Bursledon. By 1154, the list had been widened to include income from 'Ferreham, Nuctesllyng, Mellebroc, Twyfordia, Henton, Alwarestoke, Extona, Husseborne, Wytecherche, Chylboltona, Wodehaye, Awelsona, Wyeneya, Stocktona, Ovytona'. It is a comparatively easy task to bring these names into modern spelling. A list prepared for the Attorney-General in 1853 of lands presented to St Cross in 1132 contains the parsonages of Hurstbourne, Whitchurch, Twyford, Owslebury, Fareham, chapelry of Freefolk, five small properties in Winchester, Great Priestwood, Pilwood, land tax from free farm rents, manor of Ashton, 15 rectories, tithes of the demesne of Waltham, vicarages of Hurstbourne, Owslebury, Fareham and Twyford. The apparent duplication of vicarages and parsonages is because the parsonage was the actual dwelling place and the vicarage was the living. All these lists only serve to stress the wide area over which the influence of St Cross was spreading. In time, St Cross received income from 20 parishes in the Winchester diocese, two in Salisbury diocese and one in Lincoln. Apart from churches and chapels, other benefits accrued. 'Southensea' in Sussex was expected to provide three dolphins per year. This was later commuted to a payment of £4 annually, at a time when a headmaster in Leicestershire was being paid £6 each year, and the Master at the Hospital was receiving £8. They must have been first class dolphins! Most of the area known as 'Berewicke' was in the hands of St Cross. The name can mean barley farm at the edge of the town—it would be nice to think that the barley was used to produce spirits to go with the wine and ale so freely doled out at the Hospital. These grants were not just on paper only.

In 1401, de Campeden was involved in a struggle with Lord Amaury de St Amand over the ownership of the hay from three meadows called 'Bowmede, Depemede, and Woodendemede', which he claimed he had taken from de Campeden for 'Seyntecrossemede'. What was more, the Seyntecrossemede had more hay and so de Campeden had the better of the deal. It was decided that de St Amand was right. St Cross now wished to make sure that the tithes for the hay came to the Hospital. In 1404 the villagers of Twyford were excommunicated for not meeting their obligation. This was, of course, a very harsh punishment, in an era when all life revolved around the church. It also shows the influence of the Foundation, in that the Church hierarchy was willing to act so strongly on its behalf. The villagers appealed against the sentence, and the matter dragged on until 1408, when the Bishop of Winchester acted as arbitrator, and decided that only some villagers were bound to pay the tithe.

All this provided income, but the ambitious charitable scheme and building plans of Henry de Blois demanded capital. It was this lack of money, linked with quarrels between Bishops of Winchester and the Knights of St John that kept the church from completion. In the first stage of building, ending in about 1170, the eastern end of the church, plus the sacristy and transepts, was completed. As this left a large part (where a nave should be) open to the winds, a temporary wall was built across the chancel steps to mark an end to the building. Not only were Henry's plans ambitious, he was also a perfectionist. The original South Chapel (now the Lady Chapel) and the first North Chapel (now known as the Peace Chapel), were clearly completed by different master masons although at much the same period. The vaulting is quite different in one from the other. This may well be a sign of that perfectionism, in that perhaps Henry sacked the mason who did not satisfy him. Of course, there are totally mundane solutions, such as the death of one builder and his replacement by a new man, or an attempt to speed things up by having the two chapels built at the same time by different masons. Incidentally, in the strings above the arches in the nave, built in the last stage between 1320 and 1340, the Master Mason who took over in 1320 included a bunch of leaves and grapes to show the point at which he took over. He didn't intend to be blamed for his predecessor's faults and was proud of his own work!

Henry undoubtedly thought often and long of his charity in Sparkford. He had seen the uncertainties of the domestic scene, and may well have come to the conclusion that the long-term survival of St Cross could best be ensured by the protection of some international, rather than national, body. Besides, an international group would perhaps be able to provide some of the capital he needed.

Crusades were an important feature of medieval life. In the 1150s, an Englishman, Gilbert, Bishop of Lincoln, was organising a crusade against the Moors of Africa. Lincoln was a diocese which already provided income for St Cross. Amongst the many groups of knights who were preparing to set out for the Holy Land were the knights of the Order of St John. They were a wealthy and powerful body, with links all over the Christian world. It must have been very tempting to see them in the rôle of protectors. At any rate, in 1151 Henry dedicated his charity 'to the providence of God and the administration of the venerable in Christ, the Lord Raymund, Master of the Hospital of Jerusalem, and his brethren, in regular succession for ever'.

The Knights of St John, no doubt attracted by the rich endowments of St Cross, readily accepted the burden. Used as we are to thinking of St John's as being those ambulance people who look after us at fêtes and football crushes, it is hard to grasp the significance of the knights at that time. All members were bound by monk-like vows, and were first established to look after pilgrims to the Holy Land. After all, their title was Knights of the Hospital of St John of Jerusalem, better known by the shortened version of The Hospitallers. By the 12th century they had become, first and foremost, warriors. A recent estimate has suggested that they spent the equivalent of almost fifty million

7 *Eastern end of church, interior.*

8   *Modified arms of the Kingdom of Jerusalem as used by St Cross, from a window at south-west end of church*

9   *Arms of kingdom of Jerusalem above current cross of St Cross, from a downpipe outside the ambulatory.*

pounds at 1994's value in building castles in the Holy Land. Their annual bill to maintain them, again converted roughly to 1994 figures, was about two and a half million pounds. Additionally, they kept their own fleet in the Mediterranean to patrol the sea lanes so that crusaders could reach the Holy Land without let or hindrance. Obviously, they could call upon, and would need to spend, immense sums of money. They had a specific use for the church at St Cross. Travellers to the crusades, whether in France, Spain, the Holy Land, or the eastern states of Europe, spent their last night in England, before embarking at Southampton, praying in a side chapel at St Cross. This is first recorded by a small band of knights in 1189. The chapel they used was the area joining the sacristy to the nave, and is now situated behind the modern organ.

Bishop Henry must have felt that he had secured the immediate present and the long term future of his charity. A new building programme was started in 1160. The Knights of St John had helped in the victories that led to the foundation of the Latin kingdom of Jerusalem. Now the brethren at St Cross adopted the badge of that kingdom, in compliment to the knights, as theirs also. The arms of the king were 'Argent, a cross potent between four plain crosslets or' which means a large silver cross formed from what looks like four T's meeting in the middle, with four small gold crosses, set one to each arm. These five crosses signified the five wounds of Christ. In the western window in the south aisle of the church, these arms are displayed, but the crosslets are in silver to differentiate them from the king's arms. Eventually, St Cross dropped the crosslets and now uses just the one central cross. This is worn on the uniforms of all members of the original foundation. Their uniform is a black cloak and hat, reminiscent of the type worn by ordinary men of the 12th century.

This vision of safety and certainty proved to be illusory. The international duties of the order tended to lessen their ability to be active protectors of St Cross. By 1171, the building programme had ceased, and the church lay but part finished. Henry de Blois died in 1173, to be succeeded as Bishop of Winchester by Richard Toclyve, or Richard of Ilchester. Almost immediately, he began an inquiry into the various institutions within his see. St Cross was, according to its original charters, in 'the canonical justice of the Bishop of Winchester'. The 1151 deed passed the administration of the Hospital to the Knights of St John. Richard wished to see what that administration had achieved. Knowing that the building programme had ceased, he felt that there were probably questions to be answered. Here was a charity fast approaching its 50th anniversary, yet it still had no completed House of God for its worship.

Richard's investigations showed that, however splendid the Knights of St John were in looking after pilgrims to the Holy Land, they were not truly considering the welfare of their charges at St Cross. The Bishop did not have the close royal connections of his predecessor, but he did have an advantage as a churchman. Two years previously, the struggle between Henry II and Archbishop Thomas à Becket had ended in the disastrous murder of Thomas in Canterbury Cathedral. Richard had been one of the clerics who had urged the King to oppose Thomas and had, in fact, been excommunicated for his attitude. Henry had learned that it was dangerous to tangle with the Church. By 1173, Becket had been canonised, and an order of knights, St Thomas of Acre, had been founded. No doubt the crusading Knights of St John knew of this order and may even have fought alongside them. In the side chapel at St Cross in which traditionally the crusaders prayed, wall paintings, including a scene of the martyrdom of Thomas, now faced any who knelt at its altar in the arch on the east wall. There are still faint signs of the painting there and, with the eye of faith, it is possible to discern the story of Becket's murder. In 1971, this series of wall paintings was expertly examined by E. Clive Rouse. His description reads:

Top Row: At the top centre is a quatrefoil which evidently had a seated figure of Christ in Majesty, not a Head of Christ as had been previously suggested. The quatrefoil was up-held by four (not two) angels. The spandrels are too fragmentary for any suggestion to be made as to what they may have contained.

Upper Row: This row had previously been described as a Life of St Thomas of Canterbury (Thomas a Becket), but recent work has disclosed a completely different interpretation. From left to right:

(1)   destroyed.
(2)   Martyrdom of St Thomas, clearly identified by mitre on altar, kneeling figure, 2 swords and bear's head on the shield of one of the murderers, Robert Fitzurse.
(3)   Martyrdom of St Lawrence, the Saint being pressed down by a tormentor onto a gridiron with fire beneath, onlookers in the background.
(4)   (central panel) largely destroyed.
(5)   A naked male figure strung up between posts, probably with tormentors on each side. This suggests one of the scenes in the Life and Martyrdom of St George.
(6) & (7)   Defaced beyond recognition.

Lower Row: The whole of the lower panels consist of a Passion Cycle. Reading from the left:
(1)   Fragmentary, but probably Christ before Pilate.
(2)   The Scourging.
(3)   Carrying the Cross.
(4)   (centre panel) Crucifixion.
(5)   Entombment.
(6)   Fragmentary, but probably Resurrection or descent into Hell, as the vexillum can be distinguished.
(7)   Fragmentary, but probably an Ascension.
            The painting is of mid-13th century date with very fine details and elaborate and expensive colouring, including vermilion, blue, green and even gold leaf. Certainly of the Winchester school.

This places the paintings at a rather later date than that usually given them, but makes them seem even more important. Unfortunately, some twenty years later, much of the detail then recorded has disappeared.It may well be that the martyrdom painting was a *mea culpa* from Bishop Richard for his part in opposing the Archbishop, but it was certainly a forceful reminder to the departing knights of the power of the Church. In the 19th century, a second derivation was accepted, which would make the paintings a little older. Bishop Henry de Blois had been the man to consecrate Becket as archbishop. He may therefore have had the painting done, either to remind himself of his act of consecration or to mourn its final effect. However, Rouse's work would destroy this thesis.

To the south of this arch, slightly higher up, but still on the east wall, there are signs of another painting. Again, provided you go there determined to see it as such, this is a representation of St John, standing on a hill, at the far side of the wall, whilst under him are two lines, forming a patterned edge. No other design can be deduced, but it is said that the Virgin Mary was also in the picture, being comforted after the crucifixion by St John. This may have had some sort of spatial link with the crucifixion described as on the wall above the south-east altar, or with the passion said to have been on the south wall. The idea that the area leading to the sacristy was dedicated to some special worship is further strengthened by the fact that the whole south wall was thus decorated with a crucifixion scene. As late as 1900, it could still be photographed and was at that time described as showing Christ lying on the ground after being taken down from the cross, attended by two female figures. Behind them appeared the houses of the city of Jerusalem, and in the foreground was a skull and crossbones. This painting, before the advent of the organ, could be seen from the ambulatory window into the north transept of the church, through which sick brethren might look directly at it. Careful first steps in cleaning work in 1994 have revealed tiny portions of the houses of Jerusalem and the position of one female head.

No doubt Toclyve felt that he was in a very strong position when he approached Henry II for help in dealing with the administration of the knights at St Cross. Certainly, the king himself would be extremely careful not to raise antagonism in any matter with which bishops or archbishops bothered themselves, particularly when the bishop held such an important see as Winchester.

The natural interest of the Hospitallers in crusading may have turned their minds away from St Cross, but it was crusading that produced a chance to set matters right. Pope Lucius III tried to raise the standard of a further crusade in 1184, but he did not receive much enthusiastic support. Henry II was one of the great kings of Christendom, so Lucius was anxious to have him as a crusader. Already, as part of the penance for the murder of Thomas à Becket, the King had agreed to keep a standing army of 200 in Jerusalem. To persuade him to take an even more active rôle, the Pope sent to England Heraclius, Patriarch of Jerusalem and Roger de Molins, Master of the Brethren of St John in Jerusalem. The importance of getting Henry on a crusade is shown by the bribe mentioned by Milner, writing in 1798. Henry was to be offered 'the kingdom of the Holy City and country and to present him with the keys of the sacred sepulchre, as also a consecrated banner'. This was to be a very high-powered meeting, but Richard Toclyve persuaded Henry that it was also a splendid platform on which to raise the question of the mismanagement of St Cross. Thus, despite the fact that the international question of the crusades was the major item on the agenda, St Cross was also discussed.

In deference to the distance already travelled by Heraclius, and the uncertain state of the roads in England, the meeting was held in Dover. Although the council was packed with men from Jerusalem, Bishop Richard ensured that the church was well represented also, so that the case for examining the care provided at St Cross would be adequately presented. That this was regarded as a most important discussion is apparent from the detail given of those present. 'Now this transaction took place in the year of the incarnation of Our Lord, one thousand one hundred and eighty five, the fourth before the Ides of April, in the pontificate of Lucius III, in the thirty-first year of the reign of Henry the Second, at Dover; Heraclius, the Patriarch of Jerusalem, and Roger de Molins, Master of the Brethren of Jerusalem, then being in England, being there present: there being witnesses; Henry, the illustrious King of England, Heraclius, the Patriarch of Jerusalem, John, Bishop of Norwich, Randulf de Granville, Justiciary of the Lord King in England, Herbert, Archdeacon of Canterbury, etc.' Note that the witnesses included the leading figure on the legal side of the nation, as well as representatives of the knights and the church. The King was making it clear that the agreement was to have national as well as local import.

After much argument, Henry II persuaded the knights to agree to discuss with the Bishop of Winchester the terms under which they would surrender all rights to the Hospital. In return, the Church was to grant the Hospitallers the two parishes of Morton and Hanyton. Eventually, it was decided that the Bishop should pay an annual rent of 'fifty silver marks for the sustentation of the Hospital of Jerusalem, and of the poor in Christ in that Hospital perpetually'. The Knights of St John were freed from the duty of paying annually ten marks and 'two large altar candles of ten pounds wax each' which they had hitherto owed to the monks of St Swithun's. They completely resigned all their claims to St Cross and passed it, with all its rights and duties, to the Bishop of Winchester. For his part, the Bishop added a further hundred to the poor to be fed daily by the Charity. There is no hard evidence to prove that the number of two hundred was ever reached; but if it had been, it surely met almost all the needs of Winchester's poor families, as it would probably have represented support for approaching one thousand people. Throughout the document, there is a persistent reminder that all the funds of the Hospital were to be used for charitable purposes. It was 'not lawful to convert the alms deputed for the feeding of the poor in that house to another use'. Any surplus was to be 'held in own proper hands to be ordered by such fit and honest person as he and they shall think fit'. The 'own' and 'he' were both referring to the Master. This would seem to give a shadow of substance to Bishop Richard's original suspicion that perhaps the money was being used elsewhere other than at St Cross.

Heraclius returned to Jerusalem to take up the struggle against the Turks in the disastrous campaign that led to the capture of the Holy City by the moslems. Saladin set a ransom of 100,000 dinars for the whole population, but allowed Heraclius to go free on payment of the derisory amount of 10 dinars. He fled the city with a baggage train bulging with the treasure acquired by his household. Not a dinar went towards meeting the city's ransom; apparently he did not feel it worthwhile to spend some of his wealth on saving the ordinary citizens of Jerusalem from the slave markets.

It was not long before the Order of St John began to have second thoughts about surrendering St Cross. Strictly, the institute was not St Cross, but Holy Cross—the very symbol under which all crusaders fought. Its rich endowments provided powerful reasons for wishing to be back in control. For many years, the Papacy had been involved in a struggle with the temporal power of the Holy Roman Empire. On his election as Pope in 1187, Clement III determined that he would show the earthly kings that his rights came from a heavenly king and were therefore more important than theirs. When the Knights of St John appealed to him to overturn the decision of Henry II giving St Cross to the care of the Bishop of Winchester, he was delighted. Here was a splendid hook upon which to hang the thesis of papal supremacy. As it would both enable him to reverse a decision which had been trumpeted as a king's decision, witnessed by the royal justiciar, and also to support a crusading group, he gladly intervened. The Hospital was returned to the control of Canerius, Prior of the Hospital of Jerusalem in England, as one of the first acts of his reign.

As if this were not enough, new powers were granted to St Cross. 'When there is a general interdict in the land, having closed the doors, and shut out the excommunicate and the interdicted, you may then celebrate Divine service with a suppressed voice and no bells sounding. You may also receive clerks or laymen fleeing from the secular power, freely and absolutely; and retain them in your college without contradiction from anyone.'

Nobles and any people owning land needed the services of the church, at the very least, for marriages and baptisms. Their legitimacy was an important part of the scheme of things, and dynastic marriages were the norm. St Cross was thus set up as the one place where such services could take place, even if the rest of England were to be officially outside the church. Being able to accept anyone who had offended against the laws of the land, and hold them as long as the church wished, was far beyond the accepted rules. Normally, the person taking sanctuary could remain in the church for 40 days, after which he had to surrender to the king's law, and then quit the kingdom. Here at St Cross, a fugitive could apparently remain for ever. Moreover, as he could stay in any part of the 'college', he could move around, and receive food and drink—perhaps even as one of the hundred poor! Pope Clement III was in effect saying that he had placed St Cross above both the spiritual and temporal laws of the land.

Richard I succeeded to the throne in July 1189 whilst he was in France, came to England in August, and left it for his crusade in December. Thus, in four months only, he had to organise his kingdom so that he could safely leave it and use it as a style of bank to finance his wars in the Holy Land. It was perhaps part of the politics of the time that led him to take action over St Cross in the short time in which he was in England. Although primarily a crusader, Richard was also a king. He fully supported the rights of the Hospitallers to St Cross, but did not entirely appreciate the way in which the Pope had over-ridden the king and the king's law. Now he wished to make it clear that what was done was done because the king said so. He called a meeting which was sufficiently important to include David, brother of the King of Scotland, the Archbishop of Canterbury and a whole list of bishops and earls. Before them, he issued a Royal Charter confirming the surrender of St Cross to the knights. It stressed the charitable aims of the foundation, the apparent neglect of which had led to the attempt to remove the Knights of St John from control. However, the existence of Mammon was acknowledged in the grant 'to God and St John the Baptist, and the Brethren of the Hospital of Jerusalem, the House of the Holy Cross near Winchester, with all its appurtenances, —in churches and lands, in wood and plain, in meadows and pastures, in waters and mills, in ways and paths, and in all other places and in all other things, with all their liberties and free customs'.

Thus, the knights became freeholders, and it would be extremely difficult to part them from their possessions. Unfortunately, the freehold was not specifically tied totally to charity. As long as the aims of looking after the 13 men and the hundred poor could be met, then any excess income was presumably at the disposal of the knights. This was to be the beginning and root of a problem which plagued St Cross until the 19th century.

The Bishops of Winchester did not give up the fight tamely. They continually claimed that the full intentions of the founder were not being met and that some of the money which ought to have gone to charitable use was not so doing. In 1197, Celestine III, who had been elected Pope in 1191 at the age of 85, ordered a commission of enquiry into the whole affair. Richard had returned to England after his captivity in 1194, spent enough time in England to be re-crowned in Winchester, and went off once more on a crusade, never again to come to England. This commission, therefore, could not be royal, but was ecclesiastical.

Celestine appointed the Bishops of London and Lincoln, and Hugh, Abbot of Reading, to be the commissioners. Gilbert de Vere, Prior of the Order in England, and Godfrey de Lucy, Bishop of Winchester, were ordered to appear before them at Windsor. The date fixed was 'on the morrow of the Sunday on which the Cantate Domino is sung'. In those days, dates were often named from the anthem or introit sung on the Sunday— hence *cantate domino*. After some argument, the commission decided that the Knights of St John should give up all their rights of every type in St Cross. In return they would receive an annual payment of £30 per year, which was to be used to help the poor in Jerusalem or for some other purpose in England.

No doubt the Knights of St John took a quick look at their balance sheet for St Cross, and decided that £30 annually scarcely represented a good swap. They would also have felt very diffident about defying a ruling by the commissioners, who were, after all, the direct representatives of the Holy Father, the Pope. So they did what any good Englishman would do in the circumstances—they temporised. They pointed out that such an important issue as this would have to be confirmed by their Preceptor, Garcia de Lycia, who just happened to be out of England. Two messengers were sent to make contact with him.

Months passed, with no answer from Garcia to the commissioners. They began to get a little restless and demanded that the Hospitallers produce an answer at once. Sadly, they regretted they were unable to do so. Of the two messengers sent 'one of whom stayed behind in parts beyond the sea, and the other being returned, fell into such sickness that he was not in his senses, and therefore they could not be certified by him'. In the modern sense, it might have been more appropriate to say that they certified him as he was now mad. What fleshpots, one wonders, had persuaded the first man to stay away, and had excess of the same fleshly joys maddened the second man? What seems more likely is that the answer produced would have caused annoyance to the powerful commissioners and the English knights were not prepared to give it.

This was too much for the commissioners. As papal representatives in what was largely an issue for the Church, they had very wide powers. Even so, they took advice from English lawyers and then 'relieved the said Bishop of Winchester from all interference by the said Knights of the Hospital of St John in Jerusalem touching the said House of the Holy Cross ... concerning the exhibition of the poor and their support'. Thus the Bishop of Winchester regained control of the Charity, with the backing of the Pope and the lawyers of England.

There still remained some cause for argument. The knights were relieved of all matters concerning the poor and their support, but it was not crystal clear whether all the endowments went too. If the support of the poor could be continued with, say, half the endowments, the knights felt justified in claiming the rest.

Two years later, in 1199, John succeeded to the throne. He was not the universal choice, many people preferring the claims of his nephew, Arthur. He therefore set out to win the support of any powerful group he could influence. One such group was the Knights of St John. When they appealed to him, he at once issued a royal charter confirming them in possession of St Cross. King John was never on very good terms with the Church, so he was no doubt pleased to be able to help its opponent in one cause. John's actions later caused the Pope to place England under an Interdict and eventually to excommunicate the King, when the privileges granted to St Cross by Clement III must have been of considerable value.

Certainly, the issue of who controlled St Cross was not finally decided. Quietly, the Bishop of Winchester waited his chance. It came in 1204. The Mastership of the Hospital fell vacant, and the knights did not at once make an appointment. Peter des Roches, Bishop of Winchester, did not hesitate. He nominated Alan de Stoke as Master. 'Wherefore we, being desirous to take heed that the distribution of alms to be made to the Poor of Christ by the constitution of the Lord Henry the Bishop, in the House of St Cross, Winchester, may not be defrauded or perish, have elected Mr. Alan de Stoke, whom we know to be a prudent and faithful man, and have committed the cure of the said House with the appurtenances to have and to hold freely, and quietly, and peaceably for the whole time of his life, saving to us and to our successors our authority and dignity therein. And, in testimony of this appointment, we have made to him the present charter confirmed with our seal.'

There are a number of important points to note in this appointment. First is the fact that de Stoke was installed under the charter and seal of the Bishop at a time when officially the knights had control, yet the knights made no move to oppose it. This would tend to show that the knights had given up the struggle. Second, the appointment is a cure (care) of a building, rather than an ecclesiastical cure of souls. Indeed, the bishops regularly specified that the appointment was without cure of souls—'*sine cura animorum*'. Third, it is for life, and presumably a Master could not be dismissed for bad behaviour. Finally, there is the recurrent insistence upon looking after the 'Poor of Christ'—the major point at issue between Bishop and knights.

Effectively, de Stoke's appointment ended the long struggle between the Knights of St John and the Bishop. However, it was not until 1303 that the Hospitallers, in the person of their Prior, William de Tochdale, formally gave up their claim to St Cross to John de Pontissara, Bishop of Winchester. Even so, they could not be persuaded to release the muniments and records. It took all the energy and determination of Bishop Wykeham to wring them from their stubborn hands in 1379.

CHAPTER III

Building

The influence of the Charity in the area is shown on the map. The village was Sparkford, and the Hospital was the hospital of the Holy Cross. It had become known as St Cross, and the village, dominated by the huge building, followed suit. All that is left of the title Sparkford now is the name of roads such as Sparkford Close.

Even though the Knights of St John had given up St Cross, they left a permanent mark on it. The cross derived from their crusader kingdom is worn by the brethren of the original Foundation. High in one of the windows of the south transept, a simplified cross of St John rests above the head of a saintly image, probably St Gregory. St John appears in the east window glass. He is also said to be a figure just seen in the east wall by the sacristy. In the north chapel, remains of a wall painting, which John Hardacre identifies as being of very high class early 13th-century work, may show St John amongst other disciples.

A period of building activity in the church followed Henry II's award in 1185. Outside, the only difference that would have been noted up to 1200 was that the south wall of the east part of the nave aisle was extended by one bay. Internally, a new temporary dividing wall was built, closing off the crossing. Windows, most of them unglazed as would be quite normal, were completed. One of the special features of St Cross is that all the surrounds of the windows vary from each other. Most are based upon the traditional dog-tooth pattern and its later development of nail-head. In the north transept, there is the famous 'bird's beak' window where the mason has carved birds' heads all the way round. The pattern is probably unique in England, being naturalistic rather than monstrous as others are. It would seem to owe more to Angers in France than England, and may be the result of de Blois retiring for some years to Cluny, and bringing back with him both French workmen and French architectural ideas. Next to it, the south side of the window has more of an angle than the north, so that the early light on Holy Cross Day in September is directed on to the first pillar in the nave. Here, there was a statue of the Virgin Mary, and the sun's rays lit her before anything else. In 1650, the 'idolatrous' statue was removed, to be replaced much later with a simple cross of St Cross. Brother Holmes and Brother Heavens, current members of the Hospital Foundation, both testify from personal experience that the early light still falls first direct on to the cross. The Virgin Mary was especially revered because of her apparent connection with Henry de Blois, the milkmaid and the foundation of the Charity.

10 *'Bird's beak' pattern around outer shell of window in north transept.*

11   *Window in north transept throwing first light of Holy Cross day on the cross (previously statue of Virgin Mary). Note splayed south side of window.*

Along the exterior of the nave, the windows show the time elapsed in the building of the church. The most easterly is round-headed and plain, of the late Norman style. Next is of similar style, but with a hood moulding as the early Gothic style makes its appearance. Finally, the western one is pointed, complete with hood moulding and flanking pilasters. This is typical of the later Gothic style. Even the buttresses individually show the work of different masons. Easterly, the first one just seems to broaden the wall. In the middle, the buttress projects slightly and has what looks like one step in it. To the west, the whole buttress projects clearly and has two apparent steps.

The brethren, Master, and any of the workers who lived on the site, still had their dwellings in the south field, beyond what is now the boundary of St Cross. It was, of course, normal for dwellings to be south of the church in monastic buildings, so it would have been natural to have started building in this manner. However, it is important to realise that this was certainly no monastic establishment.

All this activity for 15 years exhausted either the funds available or the masons, and the work ceased once more in about 1200. Some quarter of a century later, the workers came back. This time, the final shape of the church was revealed, with the completion of the nave, without the great west window. Even this stage was not reached without difficulty. In 1255, Bishop Aethelmar appealed to the people of Winchester for funds to

12 *West end of church, interior.*

13 *A group of brothers from about 1980. The current Senior Brother (Brother Murphy) is at the back on the right. Note the cross badges of the Hospital Foundation and the round badges of the Beaufort Foundation.*

complete St Cross. He was supported in this by appeals from the Bishops of London and Ely to their clergy and congregations. It must be assumed that they were successful, as it was at approximately this date that St Cross emerged in its present dimensions. The roof, however, was left thatched. There was still work to be done inside, including the providing of the west window, but this was not done for another 70 years, in the period from, say, 1320 to 1340. On either side of the great west door are carved heads, holding up the arch. One is said to be Edward III, scowling across at the other, Bishop Orleton, whose nomination he strongly opposed. This would fit in with the dates mentioned. Until this last phase, the main entrance was through a door in the north west of the church, as is now the case. There were stone seats for the brethren to sit on in the porch area. A stone sill forms the threshold from the porch into the church. This had to be cut away to allow brethren to step over it, as it was too steep in its original form for the old men to step over easily. Its shaping has led to the much more pleasing story that it has been worn down by centuries of worshippers stepping on it. The wear of worshippers entering is, however, seen on the steps leading down from the grounds into the porch. Above the porch was a small cell, measuring approximately 11 feet by 9 feet. This was the accommodation provided for the chaplain. It had a narrow slit window looking darkly into the west end of the church. Opposite this slit was a much larger window, facing towards where Beaufort's Tower now stands, designed to bring in light and air, and from which the chaplain could see the world outside. The room was approached via a narrow staircase and passageway leading into the very wall of the church at its north-western corner. Clearly, it must have been a somewhat dim, cheerless and cramped home.

With this stage, St Cross could at last be said to have been completed, within a time span of about of two hundred years. Roughly, the church measures 40 metres from east to west, 35 metres across the transepts, reaches up to about 18 metres in the nave and 24 metres in the tower. All in all, it is a considerable building and perhaps needed a long time for completion. Nevertheless, its slightly larger sister, the Cathedral, with rather less internal problems to vex it, reached the same stage in 14 years.

This piecemeal development is another reason for stating boldly that the church was intended only for the poor men of the Charity and their servitors. For most of the period in which it was being built, it would have been difficult to fit in just the brothers, let alone anyone else!

There was now at least a recognisable edifice on site. In 1260, it was used as the place in which, 'before many magnates', an argument about paying of customs between Winchester and Southampton was settled. Each city felt that it should have special privileges with reference to the duties of the other. St Cross was chosen not only because it was an important place, but also because it could be regarded as an independent locality. As part of the soke, it might well be considered to be outside the control and law of the city. Luckily, the serene atmosphere of the Hospital helped to produce a peaceful settlement of the problem, with both cities allowing each other's citizens freedom from tolls.

Apart from the fact that the bishop now had the right to appoint Masters, the monks of Winchester had certain financial benefits from the establishment. In 1204, several grants of Godfrey de Lucy are recorded. Amongst them is 'Furthermore, from the House of St Cross he has granted them ten silver marks to clothe the poor, provided that at the end of the year enough be left over of the rents of the house from the sufficient and honourable upkeep thereof'. The monks were to use the 10 marks for the benefit of the poor only if the Hospital were properly maintained. There was a grey area, in that no-one could define what was 'the sufficient and honourable upkeep thereof'. Innocent IV made a further grant from St Cross to the monks in 1243, which was a simple rent of 10 marks per year.

Inside St Cross, there were several altars. Of course, the high altar, under the east window, was the centre of devotion. Each of the side chapels, to the north and south, had its own altar. The south chapel was dedicated to St John the Baptist, and there was also an altar to St John the Evangelist. Presumably the patronage of the Knights of St John had encouraged this doubling up of St Johns. In addition, there are five others which have been identified. These are named as St Ursula and the 11,000 virgins, St Stephen, St Sitha, all dedicated in 1388, St Katharine (this last one being dedicated in 1386), and St Thomas, in the south transept, with its wall painting of his martyrdom. St Ursula and her companions (the number varies with the telling) fled from the importunities of a British prince, escaped to Germany, but were martyred on the banks of the Rhine. The Knights Hospitallers gave directions for building a splendid shrine to her at Bruges. This connection suggests a certain reverence for her amongst the knights, and may well be the reason for the altar in St Cross. This multiplicity of altars was perfectly normal in the churches of the time.

As the 13th century closed, so the fashion for crusades ended. No longer did warriors spend their last night before commencing their journey to the Holy Land, in prayer at a transept altar of the Hospital church. Instead, the altar now came to be used by pilgrims coming from the continent to visit St Thomas' tomb. Landing at Southampton, they spent their first night after disembarking, in prayer at St Cross, at that same altar with its appropriate wall painting of the martyrdom of Becket. Pilgrims no doubt also received the travellers' dole of bread and wine before going on their way. It was usual for them to leave a little something for their hosts, as a thank you for a night's rest and food. In the light of the history of St Cross, it is quite likely that this became a 'perk' of the Master.

When the first building stage was completed, only the area immediately in front of the high altar had been paved. It was not thought necessary to provide firm footing for the congregation. As further extensions were built, the floor remained in a primeval state of hard packed earth. During the 13th century, much of the floor was tiled, using patterns similar to those found in Winchester Cathedral, Romsey Abbey, Christchurch and Beaulieu Abbey. There is so much similarity that it is suggested that they all perhaps come from the same kiln, in either Poole or Romsey. These tiles are encaustic, where the pattern is stamped in, filled in with coloured clay, covered with glaze and then baked. There are very many designs at St Cross. A double-headed eagle probably is linked to Richard of Cornwall, whose emblem it was. Of interest is the fact that he was a great benefactor of Beaulieu Abbey, and it has been suggested that this pattern came to the Hospital because the kiln made too many for the Abbey! Richard may also be commemorated in the eagle holding a scroll carved on the side of the credence table, and the label visible in the wall above it, for he was entitled to this insignia as a royal son. Another design is two monkeys, the bearings of the family of St John of Basing—a left-handed link to the Hospitallers.

14 *Tiles with the motto 'Have Mynde'.*

Included also are the lion, as the symbol of Christ the Redeemer, the dragon, representing sin, the dove for peace, and the *fleur de lys* for purity. Many are purely decorative and are simply the result of a worker having fun and taking pleasure in his craft. The tiling was completed in about 1390, and the tiles now on the east wall of the north transept, bearing the Hospital's adopted motto of 'Have Mynde', date from this time.

Symbols abounded throughout the church, for those prepared to see them. For instance, around the base of the north-west nave pillar, the carvings represent, in plant life, between them The Fall of Man (forbidden fruit), Baptism (water plant), Purity (lily), and Paradise (a victor's palm). There is even, just inside the church, in the bosses of its ceiling by the entrance door, a symbol of a religion even older than Christianity—the Green Man.

15 *The Green Man from the ceiling at the north-west end of the church.*

Most of the windows have steps below the glass or the opening for glass. These were used to provide light, as there was no central lighting at first. On each step, a number of the old-style stone lamps were placed. At the end of the 19th century, some of these lamps still survived. They were roughly brick-size with two hollows for thick wicks which had fat pressed tightly around them, and they must have produced a smelly and smoky light. It should be remembered that not much light was needed within a church as long as it was possible to see the way around, as probably only the priests, clerks and scholars would be able to read and wish to follow a service in a book. For their needs, lights in the choir area would suffice, and here candles and candlesticks were provided.

In the extensive gardens there was a fish pond and a dovecote. With the meatless days imposed on establishments connected with the church, and demanded from all others, the fish pond was only to be expected. This at least supplemented the supply provided by a river, full of fish, running less than a hundred yards from the Hospital wall. Presumably, it was thought that neither the old men who were brethren nor the servants should be put to the extra effort of going out into the meadows. Equally, having a fish pond within the walls did ensure a supply to the inmates alone which could not be taken away from them.

The dovecote is a little more interesting. Pigeons were regarded as a source of food, and the cotes were places where they were both bred and taken for the table. Usually, such shelters were the prerogative of the lord, as the pigeons made a nuisance of themselves by flying out and feeding on the crops in the peasants' fields. Here, then, was perhaps a recognition of the Master of St Cross, who controlled wide acres, as a member of the gentleman class. A last remnant of the building can be seen in the bay in the north-east corner of the garden wall.

Clearly in the 13th century, Winchester, and Sparkford with it, was an agricultural and cloth centre. There are hints that the Hospital of St Cross tried to earn its own living, regardless of its rich endowments. In the accounts for the great St Giles' Fair for 1362, it is noted that the ground rents received are lower than usual because of a pestilence, probably another type of Black Death. Amongst the rents lost are two for 20 pence each for two shops run by St Cross. From this it may be assumed that St Cross regularly had two shops in the St Giles' Fair, though it cannot be guessed what goods were sold there. In the time of King John, St Cross paid an 'Aquagium', or water rate, of £1 for its water mill. By 1213, the Hospital also held the mill at 'Draiton' and paid £4 a year for the privilege. Almost certainly, these mills were for grain or malt. It later leased a fulling mill at £1 per year. Presumably St Cross then had trade both in grain and cloth. By about 1480, the grain mill had been levelled to the ground. Nevertheless the brethren were still expected to pay the same rent for the water running through their grounds as an 'aquagium' was deemed to be still due, even if the mill was not at work. Their rooms were served by the streams in the style of a very primitive waste disposal, though what the waters further downstream from them were like does not bear thought!

Records of the Masters of St Cross at this period are scanty. Robert of Limesia is really only known through his appearance in the papal confirmation of his office and his witnessing an episcopal document. Similarly, William, who was Master at least in 1171 and 1172, is known only as witness to two grants made by the Bishop of Winchester in those years. One charter is appropriately of churches 'to the sacrist and the Hospitallers of Jerusalem', the then 'owners' of St Cross. The second grant may perhaps give a clue to the date of the end of Robert of Limesia's time as Master. On 6 August 1171, William witnessed a document restoring lands to the monks of St Swithun. They include 'Burclere' which was included in the lands whose restoration Robert witnessed, and 'Merdone' which had been specifically excluded at that time. Both these restorations were made towards the end of Bishop Henry's life (he died in 1173), when he was searching his conscience and trying to have all matters clear, so that his soul might rest in peace after death. The addition of Merdone in the second document witnessed by William may be the result of a short period of mature thought which led him to feel that he should not really have excluded it in the first place. Also, in the second restoration charter, Henry acknowledged that he held the lands unjustly, having admitted to taking them into his hands in the earlier document witnessed by Robert. Both comments would seem to be typical of a powerful 12th-century man coming to the end of his life and hoping to purge his sins. The two documents may thus very well have followed closely one upon the other. It is possible, therefore, that William succeeded Robert de Limesia in 1171. Robert is known only in that Bishop Toclyve collated him in 1185. Alan de Stoke is documented in his institution but nothing else. About 1235, a Humphrey de Myles is noted as Master. He was succeeded in 1241 by Henry de Secusia.

At this time, there was a struggle between monks and king over who should be Bishop of Winchester. Henry III wanted William of Valentia, but the monks elected Walter de Ralegh. When Walter attempted to enter the city, he found the gates locked against him by the King's order, so he placed Cathedral and city under an interdict. One of the priests who opposed him fiercely was Henry de Secusia. As the office of Master of St Cross was vacant, Henry III nominated him to the post, declaring that there was no bishop available to exercise the rights of patronage. *The Victoria History of Hampshire* says that he later went on to become Cardinal Bishop of Ostia and 'one of the most famous canonists of the middle ages'. He was followed by three Masters, about whom only the names are known.

Peter de Sancta Maria took office in 1289. There are some grounds for suggesting that Sancta Maria as a surname was a mis-writing of the word 'Seymour', a family who held lands in the area, and one branch of which was later to provide a queen of England. There would be nothing unusual in a scion of a noble house holding an important post within the church. It was during his Mastership that the church may be said to have been completed though there was still work to be done. At least the full area was now usable. His rôle as a priest outside St Cross is underlined by the fact that he was Archdeacon of Surrey. At his death in 1295, he was buried in a marble coffin, set in what was once a highly coloured and decorated alcove in the easternmost bay of the north aisle. In Victorian times, workmen accidentally broke the Purbeck marble cover of the tomb. For a moment, the body of de Sancta Maria lay whole and complete, staring up at the labourer. Then, as the air reached it, the body dissolved, leaving just the cope to show what had once been there. It is at least a wonderful compliment to the ability of the 13th-century masons that the tomb remained totally air-tight for the next six hundred years, thus preserving the body. For the superstitious, the fact that the body had for so long been kept from decaying was a clear sign that de Sancta Maria was some sort of saint in fact as well as surname.

As St Cross grew, so did Sparkford. Originally a small vill with a few houses clustered on what is now Back Street, it became more widely spread as the years went by. More houses were needed, if for no other reason than that those who worked in St Cross had to live somewhere. Each part of the Soke which had sufficient inhabitants had its own policeman or 'alderman'. Certainly, by 1300 Sparkford had reached that status, for the Cathedral records show the aldermanry of Sparkford paying 12 pence as a fine—no small amount at that time. Even more indicative of the growth of Sparkford is the note in 1327 that Edward 'le draper' of Sparkford was assessed at 20 shillings, the second highest in the whole of Winchester.

CHAPTER IV

'...to the known dilapidation of the goods...'

By the 13th century, both the Master and Hospital of St Cross held positions of considerable importance. The Master controlled a large income and provided work for the majority of the people who lived in the nearby village. Beyond that, his influence spread across the city of Winchester because of his provision of food and drink for the poor, and yet further still, through the Wayfarers' Dole, to travellers from all over the land. St Cross obtained both privileges and duties as a result.

The Hospital had a splendid park, consisting of meadows sweeping down to the River Itchen. When these were mowed, the men employed to do the work were able to claim a jack of beer. Jacks are simply leather jugs, waxed to make them waterproof. If they were tarred at the base, they were black jacks. Their capacity varied considerably from area to area. In the kitchen at St Cross, there are two jacks, each said to be capable of holding two gallons. Although these containers are certainly of no date before the 15th century and may even be as late as 17th century, it is probable that the earlier jacks held the same amount. They were, of course, big and heavy, and to lift them involved using much elbow power—hence the expression 'more power to your elbow'.

A privilege to the brothers was that of 'lop and top'. When a tree in the park land fell or was cut down, the brethren had the right to take off any side branches (lop) and remove the upper part of the tree (top). Of course, some of the brethren were too old or infirm to take advantage of this. They did not suffer, as the more active men wielded the saw and billhook on their behalf. Generally, there was a very broad interpretation as to where the top and the lop extended, and quite large logs were carried away. This was a much prized privilege, as it provided free heating in the brethren's accommodation for much of the winter. The custom continued almost into the 20th century.

As was to be expected in an institution of that time, St Cross did its best to be self-supporting. Its menus demanded considerable supplies of food. Cattle and sheep grazed the meadows, fish came from the fishpond, pigeons from the dovecote. Within the park, modern research has postulated a moated garden and orchard. Certainly, all the signs of a rampart around an area to the south of the church, within which are the marks of the first cells for the Master and brethren, do give grounds for assuming the existence of some sort of protected and cultivated area. If there were a moated garden, the water has dried up or been diverted and only an arid skeleton remains. A survey of 1401 mentions an orchard, plus a vegetable garden, the Porter's garden, the Home garden and a little 'pightle', or enclosed garden.

A moat, apart from serving as a barrier to keep out the cattle, sheep, and perhaps deer that grazed across the meadows, may have had a second purpose. The water for it must have come via a diversion from the local river and stream. Originally, the water seems to have flowed diagonally from the entrance gate, under what is now a lawn, and into the north-west corner of the supposed moat. If this is so, it had a considerable fall and would have had sufficient power to drive the mill for which St Cross paid a rent. An advantage of this would be that the mill itself would have been within the confines of the Hospital. A record of John de Campeden in 1392, which seems to refer to the present St Cross Mill, says, 'They have newly made a mill pool and two hatches with sluices and one mill away from the community, clearly to the eastern area of the mills' control'. There must, then, have been two mills, one by the Hospital and one rather more remote from it.

Two great waves of plague, known as the Black Death, swept through Hampshire in 1349 and again in 1361. Records suggest that St Cross suffered less than other parts of the county, including Winchester. Perhaps the state of hygiene in the Hospital was better than elsewhere, helped by the fact that there was a wide open space all around it and a stream flowing through and under it. Being self-supporting would mean that there would be less need to mix with the public, from whom the plague might come, than was elsewhere the case. If there were to be little or no contact with the outside world, then charities like the Wayfarers' Dole and the hundred poor must have also been cut down considerably. This might have happened naturally merely from the fact that, with so many people dying, there simply weren't the travellers passing St Cross and the poor were the first to die from the Black Death.

The promotion of Masters into the ranks of 'landed gentry' led to many abuses. These failings were not peculiar to St Cross. In 1305, Pope Clement V issued his bull, called 'Quia contingit' from the first two words in it. This drew attention to the general waste, negligence, and misappropriation in 'Houses for the reception of Strangers, Leper-Houses, Alms-Houses, or Hospitals'. As a first step, they were at once to make inventories of the goods in their care and ownership and thereafter produce an annual account of income and expenditure.

Already, in 1304, St Cross was attracting the attention of the newly installed Bishop of Winchester, Henry Woodlock. He was horrified by what he saw. There must have been considerable peculation to disturb his conscience. In 1313, Pope Clement gave special dispensation to the Bishop to appoint six clerks under the proper age. Woodlock at once appointed six young relatives, so that the income remained in the family.

The Master of St Cross was Robert Maidstone, who held at the same time two rectories and a canonry of Chichester. He had been in office since 1299. After examining the evidence before him, the Bishop issued a solemn sentence of deprivation against Maidstone. Robert was officially deprived because he held too many livings at one time. When ordered to appear before the Bishop and show the dispensations which allowed him to do so, he simply did not turn up—'Mr. Robert although often sufficiently warned, and throughout the whole day until the morrow indulgently awaited for, in no wise appeared'.

Not only did he hold in plurality but, as Woodlock said, each was 'sufficiently profitable'. To show that the Hospital was under his control, Woodlock admitted three men, Gilbert le Forester, John de Fareham, and Robert de Colynch, a priest, as brethren of the Hospital. However, it would seem that his decision to remove the Master was reversed, as documents make it clear that Maidstone was still acting as Master at least in 1316, at the end of Woodlock's episcopacy, and apparently in 1321. Papal documents, for instance, quote that he was eventually deprived on 12 June 1321. Perhaps he was able to make some sort of agreement with Woodlock and was given a second bite at the cherry. The reconciliation must have been complete, as the Bishop carried out ordinations, not in the Cathedral, but at St Cross, as well as at various times in a number of parish churches around his diocese.

Because of its splendid endowments, the post of Master of St Cross was a much sought after prize. For a short while, Edward II kept the Diocese of Winchester vacant after the death of de Sandale, who had succeeded Woodlock. Two elections of bishops were in fact set aside, before Asserio ascended the diocesan throne. In this period of vacancy, the King claimed all the rights of the Bishop, and thus had the authority to nominate the Master of St Cross. He decided to reward his clerk, Geoffrey de Welleford, with this particular plum. When Bishop Asserio was installed, he verbally agreed to accept Welleford. Soon, he had second thoughts, because, he said, Maidstone was still alive and therefore legitimately Master, since the post was a perpetual benefice, from which he could only be ejected by papal bull. The King would have none of this, and in June 1321 repeated his orders that de Welleford should be made Master. Asserio gave way, having heard of the episcopal letter of deprivation issued against Maidstone, and, at the end of June, duly collated Geoffrey de Welleford to the position. The shadow of what was to come lies in the fact that the ceremony had to be completed by a proxy, as Geoffrey had not so far visited his new charge.

The people of St Cross, villagers and brethren alike, apparently did not take kindly to the idea of an absentee Master. When Geoffrey's representative arrived to take over the Hospital on behalf of his master, the locals actively resisted and totally prevented him from doing so. A week after the ceremony, Edward II ordered the Bishop to let him know if there were any further resistance. In an attempt to please the King, the Bishop once more carried out a service of collation, still by proxy, accompanied by stern warnings of imprisonment or excommunication to anyone who opposed Geoffrey's proctor in his attempt to take over.

Next, the sheriff's bailiff went to the Hospital 'on the Friday after the Transalation of St Thomas' to discover exactly what problem, if any, existed, and to end all resistance. He reported that he had met no obstruction and that the area was quiet. A week later, the King wrote to the Bishop about the bailiff's reply: 'at which answer the king marvels, especially as it is testified before him by trustworthy men that a lay and armed force was then and still is in the house of St Cross, and that the bailiff's answer was made frivolously and derisively'. Accordingly, he ordered the sheriff to gather together a band of the county's soldiers and go himself to St Cross, expel all armed people and anyone not connected with the Charity, and to put Geoffrey de Welleford in full possession of it and its goods and chattels. Anyone who resisted the order was to be thrown into prison. Calling out the soldiers was a considerable effort, as there was no standing army, and it was a case of fetching men who owed service in return for their land, from villages across the county. Just to make sure that his will was obeyed, and that the Bishop had no way of hiding behind a higher authority, Edward issued two writs ordering the Archbishop of Canterbury to keep out of the affairs of St Cross.

Still the matter dragged on. A commission of oyer and terminer, for judges on circuit to hear and determine the case, was issued on the plea of Geoffrey de Welleford. He claimed that Robert de Maidstone and his brother Nicholas had carted off Hospital property and livestock to the value of £100–almost twenty times the Master's official salary. By November, the value had gone up to £500, including goods, chattels, muniments and charters.

Early in 1322, Bishop Asserio set up a commission to make a close inquiry into the 'theft' by the Maidstones. On 11 March, yet again by proxy, since he was still not in Winchester, Geoffrey de Welleford took the oath of canonical obedience to the Bishop, and so may be said to be truly Master of St Cross. Within five months, he was dead. Despite all the trouble, the calling out of the army, the cases involved, and three proxy collations, he never once set foot in St Cross.

Asserio's commission has produced an interesting fact. At one point, it talks of the three sisters resident in the Hospital. No other official document to that time mentions anyone other than men—brethren, priests, etc. Perhaps at some stage, three nuns had been introduced into the company to look after the old men who were, by definition, unable to look after themselves. Part of the ambulatory is called the Nuns' Rooms, but they are in a section which is of a later century. Possibly it replaced buildings with the same purpose and of an earlier date, equating with rooms for the commission's 'three sisters'.

Having been involved so much in the affairs of St Cross, Bishop Asserio no doubt knew how valuable it was. At any rate, with a true family-first attitude, he appointed his nephew, Bertrand Asserio, who was concurrently a priest of Cahors, to the post. The family link was completed at the collation of the new Master. The Bishop was absent in Rome, so the ceremony was carried out by the Vicar General, his brother Gerald. Nepotism was to be well known in St Cross, which in itself is a measure of the value of the post of Master. Several bishops of future times took advantage of their right of nomination to improve the family fortunes. Wykeham appointed his nephew, Nicholas, to manage the Hospital. Edington sent in his young nephew. Hoadly appointed his son. North likewise gave the preferment to his son.

There is no evidence that Bertrand Asserio ever actually set foot in St Cross. Apart from the post in Cahors, he also held the living of Freshwater in the Isle of Wight, and was a prebend of Salisbury Cathedral. As at St Cross, so elsewhere he seems to have been very largely an absentee. To crown his ghostlike work, in 1330 he appointed attorneys to act on his behalf, as he was going abroad for two years. At the end of the two years, he did not return, having exchanged St Cross, through the Pope, for other livings abroad.

So far, Masters had been variously appointed on the initiative of the Bishop of Winchester, the Knights of St John, and the King of England. Now it was the Pope's turn. He appointed one of his chaplains, Peter de Galiciano, as the exchange priest with Asserio. The Bishop of Winchester was not at all happy. Peter was blind, and Stratford felt him to be incapable of carrying out the office, besides not being canonically qualified. As Winchester

Cathedral's documents put it, 'a rumour has reached him that Peter de Galiciano, who claims to be warden of St Cross, has entered upon the wardenship without canonical title, to the peril of his soul'. Purely out of consideration for Peter, just as the Inquisition tortured and killed for the eternal benefit of its victims, the Bishop had to take action. It was nothing to do with the fact that de Galiciano had not vowed obedience to him! In his statement, the Bishop said: 'Master de Galiciano had misapplied the rents and profits of the House, in granting the same to suspected and foreign persons who take flight to foreign parts, to the known dilapidation of the goods of the said House, and the subtraction of alms'. It is a neat way of saying that Peter had his hand in the till: it also vaguely suggested that all would have been acceptable if the rents and profits had gone to Englishmen rather than foreigners. De Galiciano appealed first to the Archbishop of Canterbury, and then to both Pope and Archbishop, for protection. Canterbury supported him and forbade Stratford to continue with the expulsion. However, the Bishop obtained the right to bring the Master to a church court in 'St Mary de Aldermarichurche in London on the sixth law day after the Sunday on which is sung the Misericordia domini'. When the bishop's officer tried to serve this mandate on Peter, he was unable to do so. 'In accordance with his mandate he has searched for master Peter de Galiciano at St Cross and other places without success, and he begs to be excused for the present for the non-delivery of the citation.'

To defeat the effects of this attempt to escape a hearing, Stratford sequestrated all the Hospital property to the 'Rector of Wykeham', John Hyde, on 13 April 1332. Stratford did this because he was 'wishing to provide that the fruits and profits of the same House be applied to such purposes but which Master Peter de Galiciano had otherwise applied and was notoriously unfit for such custody ... he, the said Peter de Galiciano in fact and without canonical title having entered and so detains the same by most injurious occu-pation, not knowing how, or being willing to govern usefully'. Hyde was involved almost solely in the administration of the properties and goods belonging to the Charity, with little consideration for the men who lived there. As such, he did far more than any absentee Master and actually improved the financial situation at St Cross. Peter de Galiciano did not give up without a struggle. He approached Edward III, who issued a royal mandate in October 1334, to his 'beloved Serjeant, Peter de Pountiff' to go to Winchester and help Peter to collect all the rents that were due to him. This would have involved the use of armed force, in the name of the king. Once more the scene was set for a struggle between Church and state over St Cross, as in de Welleford's time. Fortunately for St Cross, de Galiciano died before the whole business became too desperate.

Hyde apparently showed no desire to continue in office, so the new Bishop of Winchester, Adam de Orleton, appointed William Edington as Master of St Cross. Edington at that time was rector of nearby Cheriton. Questions were asked as to whether the Master could also be rector of another parish. This was a question about Masters presumably made rather more acute because of what had happened to Maidstone. It was an effort by all concerned to try and make sure that there was no room for a new argument. A commis-sion was set up, in true English style, led by Prior Alexander and John of Uske, rector of Burghclere. They found that 'the custody of the House of the Holy Cross was free and exempt from all cure of souls' and that the churches 'annexed to it' were not curated. The important part for later Masters was 'that the same custody, not being curated, might be retained by a rector of a parish and that it was constituted as a perpetual benefice, to which collation might be made and secular clerks assigned to the same, and should and ought to be free from taking any oath, the making of an inventory, and the charge of rendering any account of the administration of the goods; and that the warden, after institution and induction into the corporal possession of the custody aforesaid of the goods, fruits and profits, might freely dispose thereof, without rendering any account.' So—no need for an ordained priest, no checks on how the money was received and spent, the ability to hold in plurality, and in fact a licence to do what you pleased for life once installed as Master.

Edington was, however, determined to do the job properly, and at once set to work to repair the damage of the last hundred years. An actual living, resident, and working Master had by now become something of a novelty to the brethren and St Cross as a whole. The church was still thatched, and one of his first projects was to give it a proper lead roof. To introduce light and air, he had the nave clerestory built and glazed. At the west end, he had the two pinnacles rebuilt, making them safe. Inside the church, a pulpit, given by the rector of Morestead, William Byflete, was erected. Byflete was also 'a priest of St Cross', perhaps one of the Chaplains. Sadly, the pulpit has long since been removed.

In the area of the present Porter's lodge, close to the Hundred Menne's Hall, he had a Master's lodge built, bringing it for the first time within what are now the confines of St Cross. A new hall, currently called the Brethren's Hall, was built and roofed in Spanish chestnut. It is claimed that this was the first use of that wood in England for such building work. The hall itself was intended to be the Master's Hall, though it was probably used also for communal activities. At first, it was heated by an open fire, with the smoke escaping through a hole in the roof. During the 15th century, a low hearth for an equally low charcoal fire was introduced and the hole was closed. The Hall was conveniently situated close to the kitchen and buttery.

Certainly, Edington was very energetic and spent a great deal of money on putting the buildings to rights. Contemporary accounts give a figure of over £1,000. All attempts to equate figures of expenditure with modern day amounts founder on the fact that money is spent on very different things in very different ages. However, it would not be unrealistic to suggest that this £1,000 is equivalent to about £500,000 in 1994.

After all this expenditure, a slight niggle arose as to whether Edington had any right to be Master. Bishop Orleton thought it best to have the matter clarified by the Pope. He admitted that he may have acted wrongly in giving the post to William de Edington in succession to Peter de Galiciano. He had not realised that Peter was a chaplain to Clement V, and that therefore for that time the appointment to the Hospital lay with the Pope. However, in the 11 years since he took over the position, Edington had spent more than £1,000 in repairing the buildings and generally improving the lot of the poor. Orleton asked the Pope to validate William's appointment and thereby to recognise all the good he had done. Clement VI graciously agreed and sealed his agreement by remitting all the money he had received from St Cross.

Such an energetic and capable priest was bound to be marked for preferment, and in 1345 he was appointed Bishop of Winchester, after the royal mandate for John de Veneys was withdrawn. Later still, he was offered succession to the Archbishopric of Canterbury,

16 *The Brethren's Hall showing the ancient roof timbers.*

but refused saying, 'Though Canterbury be the greater stall, Winchester be the deeper trough'.

St Cross now returned to its pattern of absentee Masters. First, the Pope, not having had his turn after de Galiciano, appointed Raymund de Pelegrini, who was his ambassador, or *nuncio*, in England. The office was then reported as worth £6 13s. 4d. per year.

The full details of the ceremony of Raymund's induction still survive.

> On the 14th day of May, A.D. 1345, after the hour of vespers, before the gate of the Hospital or House of St Cross, near Winchester, in the presence of the notary public, and other witnesses, the venerable man, Mr. Raymund Pelegrini, Canon of London, presented and exhibited certain letters apostolical:- to wit, one of grace, and another executory, of our lord the Pope, being true leaden bulls, sealed after the manner of the Roman Court, not vitiated or cancelled, but free from all error and suspicion,—to the venerable man Mr. John de London, rector of the church of Esher in the diocese of Winchester, the sub-executor concerning the provision or grace in such process together with other colleagues. The said letters apostolical, to wit, the one of grace with silken threads, and the other executory with canvass threads ... Forthwith, the said Mr. John, by the delivery of the principal door of the said Hospital, and afterwards of the bell-ropes, delivered into the hands of the said Mr. Raymund, did, by the apostolical authority committed to him, actually and effectually induct the said Mr. Raymund Pelegrini into the corporal possession of the said Hospital or House, and all its rights and appurtenances; and subsequently, the same Mr. John advancing to the high altar of the church, in fuller token of such possession, delivered and assigned to the said Mr. Raymund a book, to wit, a missal; and a chalice.

Three days later, Raymond appeared at Southwark before the Bishop of Winchester. 'The aforesaid Mr. Raymund presented and exhibited the aforesaid letters and process to the said lord William, Bishop of Winchester, and requested that he would admit him as the true Master, or Warden, of the House of St Cross. And the said Bishop, having reverently admitted the said letters, and diligently inspected them, did, as far as in him lay, admit the aforesaid Mr. Raymund.'

de Pelegrini was apparently not enamoured of St Cross, and in February 1346 resigned to take up the prebendal church of Gillingham in Dorset. Two brief interludes followed, that of Walter de Wetgang and Richard de Lutteshall. Both of these appointments were disputed in church circles and Walter's was brief enough to have escaped notice on the normal list of St Cross Masters. However, he did exist and he was nominated as Master, his collation being quoted in the later 19th-century lawsuit.

Bishop Edington now decided that the family deserved a turn, and in 1346 appointed his nephew John, a young lad of 17, with no canonical title, as Master. Papal letters show that John also held the Wardenship of Godshouse, Portsmouth, was a canon and prebendary of Lincoln, and a canon of Salisbury, with every expectation of becoming prebendary there. However, the Pope was not yet finished with St Cross. In June 1348, he made William de Farlee, who was already canon and prebend in Winchester, Romsey and Salisbury, Master of the Hospital. Not until 1349 did Edington take up the cudgels on his nephew's behalf. He pointed out to the Pope that he had already collated John. The bishop argued although he was under age for a priest and had no canonical title, he already held two benefices, so this could not be argued against him. He also asserted that nowhere in the statutes was it forbidden to appoint secular clerks. Moreover, nephew John had been appointed before William de Farlee. However clearly the bishop might hold the right of appointment, the Pope was the complete overlord of the church and his opposition could be fatal to a nomination. The Pope maintained, momentarily, his appointment of Farlee, presumably merely to show his right to do so, and then confirmed John. Thus, for most of a year in 1348 and 1349, St Cross actually may claim to have had two Masters.

This plurality of officers will scarcely have worried the papacy, which had just once more gone through a period of two popes at the same time, and was approaching its high-water mark of cloning when there would be three concurrently. It did, however, worry the Edingtons. According to Bishop Edington's documents, still extant, on 18 April 1349 he re-collated his nephew as Master of St Cross, specifically noting it as a perpetual benefice, without cure (or care) of souls. (*In beneficium perpetuum et non curatum animorum.*) It is of interest that this statement should be made publicly only after the claims of William de Farlee had been withdrawn.

Whilst John was Master, the parishioners of St Margaret, Sparkford were given permission by the bishop to hear masses and other divine services, and receive the sacraments and sacramentals in the church of St Cross. This was because the great pestilence of 1349 had reduced their numbers, and they were unable to maintain a priest or repair their church. Bishop Edington had similar trouble in the Cathedral and was forced to stop his building work through lack of labourers.

The two Edingtons were as unlike each other in their employment of the office of Master as they could be. Uncle William found the place a desert and turned it into a repaired set of buildings and an operating charity. No doubt the old gentlemen who lived within the walls greatly benefited from his work. Nephew John, taking his cue from the findings of Alexander and Uske, decided to make as much as he could as quickly as he could from the Hospital. The movables went first—cattle, corn, any easily moved musical instruments, even kitchen goods. Next, as much of the income as he could safely garner, and it was a high proportion, disappeared into his own pocket. One of his methods was to draw money for repairs which he simply did not do. The desert his uncle had found returned to St Cross. Even the Hundred Menne's Hall was allowed to fall into total disrepair. When his uncle died, and a new bishop was obviously imminent, John weighed up his chances of survival without friendly family support, decided they were not good and resigned office in 1366.

CHAPTER V
Reforming and Rebuilding

John Edington was succeeded by William de Stowell, who probably anticipated that he would be able to continue with the buccaneering policy of Edington. Instead, he found that the new Bishop, Wykeham, was making awkward inquiries. At any rate, he soon arranged an exchange to Burghclere with Richard de Lyntesford. Wykeham sanctioned the exchange, but with conditions. Before he left, Stowell was to make a full inventory of all the goods of the Hospital, present one copy to the Bishop, one to Lyntesford, and keep one for himself. To ensure that Lyntesford would not try to defraud the Hospital, Wykeham, as his ecclesiastical superior, put an order of sequestration on the new Master's goods and chattels. Any shortfall in Hospital expenditure could now be made good direct from Richard's private means.

Now that he had some idea of what it was that St Cross owned and held in 1367, Wykeham ordered an examination to discover the position in 1349 at the death of Lutteshall. Clearly the intention was to exert tight control on the revenues of St Cross. Lyntesford was not making the money from it that he had expected and his private goods were at risk if he tried any of the tricks successfully used by his predecessors. Accordingly, he made an exchange with Sir Roger de Cloune for the rectory of Campsall in Yorkshire. Strictly, this counted as a presentation by the Archbishop of York, as de Cloune was in his archdiocese. Archbishops were allowed to make one presentation into any living in the country on taking up office. They nominated the living, which was on four occasions St Cross, and waited until it became vacant, when they could then exercise their option. This continual exchange of office, together with other reports he had received, convinced Wykeham that all was not well at St Cross. As Chancellor of the country, he was, in 1370, to use his own words 'in many ways so occupied in various and difficult affairs of the king that he could not personally' carry out an investigation himself. Instead, he asked (as a man who knows he cannot be refused, asks) his ecclesiastical superior, the Archbishop of Canterbury, to discover the reasons for the exchanges. Whatever the Archbishop found, he advised that Roger be confirmed as Master, presumably not wishing to step on his brother Archbishop's toes.

De Cloune was a tough old rogue, and would have been perfectly at home with the robber barons who plagued England at the time of the foundation of St Cross. At once, he set out to enrich himself at the Hospital's expense. All movable articles that had not been disposed of by his predecessors, he sold. Once more, reports speak of corn, cattle and sheep being sent to market, and materials intended for repair turned into cash for the Master. De Cloune went one stage further than previous Masters in the matter of buildings. The Hundred Menne's Hall was in a poor state of repair, so he took it largely apart and sold the bricks and wood. One report said that he had 'the Clerken House' pulled down also, and sold that piecemeal. Perhaps this referred to the end of the cloister which came into the triple arch and sacristy as there was no evidence of a building there after this time. He even started taking down some of the brethren's quarters, to sell the bits and pieces from them. Clearly, this meant that, to de Cloune, the brethren were just a nuisance, as he could not pull down their houses whilst they were still living in them. So he turned them all out. The hundred poor could not be fed in the Hall, as he was demolishing it, so they were given scanty commons at the gate. No comment is made about the Wayfarers' Dole, but it may be assumed that it, too, was given out but grudgingly at the gate.

Wykeham could not allow such criminal activity to be carried out almost under his nose. He ordered the most recent and current Masters of St Cross—Stowell, Lyntesford and de Cloune—to come to a court at Southwark in October 1370. Here he laid down what he saw as the rules of conduct for the Hospital. All the revenue of the Hospital, except a Master's allowance of £7 4s. 6d., was to be spent on the relief of the poor. Each year, the Master was to give an account to the Bishop of what he had done, and to provide an inventory, as required by Clement V's bull of *Quia Contingit*. Moreover, the mastership was not a perpetual benefice, but was an actual office requiring residence and personal work within the Hospital. To no-one's surprise, the Masters responded with quotations from Alexander and Uske's decision. De Cloune stressed that he was at St Cross for life, and that he had no duty to explain himself to anyone. *Quia Contingit* simply did not apply, as this was not an hospital under the terms of that bull. In fact, the Master had a totally free hand in administering all the revenues, lands and goods belonging to St Cross, and his only particular task was to make a small distribution of food and drink to a small number of people both inside and outside the walls. Note the word 'small'.

Wykeham now needed to obtain evidence to support his statements. One line of attack was to prove that for a long time there had been an extensive charity, beyond anything carried out by de Cloune. Walter of Sevenhampton had for six years been Steward at the Hospital, but had moved and was, in 1373, rector of Middlemarsh and prebendary of Romsey. His evidence opened with the comment 'that many, very many, poor, weak and imbecile men are accustomed to come and collect together for the support of the alms there to be found and had regularly from day to day come and there they meet and receive the same and daily receive certain alms in such manner as is accustomed to be done in other Hospitals for poor people up to the time of Sir Roger de Cloune'. He maintained that in his time 100 poor were daily fed in the Hundred Menne's Hall, receiving five marks of coarse bread, three quarts of weak beer, enough pottage, a herring and two pilchards, or two eggs or a farthing's-worth of cheese. Thirteen poor scholars also were fed with the same fare, whilst four priests and seven poor reading boys lived in. Robert Frere was a brother of the Hospital and confirmed Walter's evidence, adding that there was a special cook, pot and ladle kept for the 100 poor. Adam Jacob, who was over eighty, had been born near the gates of the Hospital and become sacristan, holding that office for 30 years. He was equally clear about the existence of the 100 poor and the 13

17   *The brass of John de Campeden.*

brethren. Another witness said that at one time there had been an agreement to feed 200 poor, but that the extra 100 had been rejected in order to support four priests, 13 lay clerks and seven choristers. Each priest dined at the Master's table and had a stipend of 13s. 4d. Each of the clerks was entitled to a daily loaf of wheat bread, three quarts of beer, and a mess of meat or fish in the same quantity as was provided for the brothers. The choristers received bread or what was left from the Master's table, to a value of 5d. per week and were taught at the school in the Hospital. This is the first official, written evidence that has survived of a school in St Cross, although the very earliest records talk of poor scholars of St Swithun at the Hospital. The list must have been almost enough to cause de Cloune to have apoplexy, as it certainly showed a charity much bigger than any other then in operation.

For about eighteen months, hearings continued, with lawyers from both sides having a field day. Stowell and Lyntesford decided that they had had enough, and accepted the ruling. Stowell's submission included the important phrase 'and that all and singular such goods are for the use of the poor aforesaid, and not to be converted to other uses, except a reasonable and moderate support of the master or warden aforesaid'. This is a clear acceptance of the fact that the Hospital was not just something to be used to add to the comfort and wealth of the Master. Equally, this submission at least tacitly shows that the former Masters realised that all that de Cloune had done, however much he fought against it, was totally illegal. The two men were fined £100 each, half to go to the Pope and half to Wykeham's fund for reshaping Winchester Cathedral. De Stowell's submission was witnessed, amongst others, by John de Campeden, Peter le Draper and four 'literates'.

Wykeham started a suit in the courts accusing the current Master of 'Dilapidation, Dissipation and Subtraction, public and notorious, of the goods of the Hospital'. Whilst the case was being argued, the Bishop sequestered all the goods and chattels of the Hospital, appointed an assistant to control de Cloune in any actions he took, and ordered him to provide for the poor as had been usual in the past. De Cloune at once appealed to the Pope, who appointed the Bishop of London to hear the case. Not until December 1373 was a decision handed down. It stated that the Foundation was an Hospital or alms-house for 'the poor, weak and imbecile of Christ', and should always have within its doors the 13 brethren of the original Foundation. Also, the funds of the Charity were to provide for four priests, three secular clerks and 100 poor men. Certainly, the Master of the Hospital held a 'temporal office', and care must be taken that it did not confer any benefice upon anyone. Masters, present and future, had to make an inventory and account of their stewardship annually. Finally 'Sir Roger should be effectually compelled, and also by ecclesiastical censures be obliged, to maintain the ordinances of the said Hospital, as of a simple ecclesiastical benefice, according to the foundation.' In the civil law courts, de Cloune was found guilty as charged and fined £50, which the judge later reduced to £44, as compared with the other Masters' £100.

Still not giving up, de Cloune refused to accept the Bishop of London as judge, saying that the Pope had not had the full facts before him when he agreed to have the case tried. Eventually, in February 1374, it was decided that Wykeham had proved his case and that the Hospital should be administered as laid down by the Bishop of London and his commissioners. At this, de Cloune at once appealed over the Bishop's head to the Pope.

Wykeham straightaway wrote to Rome pointing out that the appeal was merely a way by which de Cloune hoped to stave off the day of his ejection and that meantime he would continue on his merry way, embezzling the goods of the Hospital.

By now, de Cloune must have realised that the sands were running out, and in January 1375 he came before the Bishop of London in a penitent state. He admitted he had been wrong, gave up his appeal, and agreed to provide an inventory and annual account to the Bishop of Winchester. He was thereupon patted gently on the head and told to go away and sin no more. Apparently he took the implied 'go away' seriously, as he is next reported as having left the country.

There was still one more loose end for Wykeham to tie up in the de Cloune affair. Like many Masters before and after him, de Cloune had appointed a deputy to do any work that might be necessary in St Cross, whilst he himself took the rich pickings. His chosen agent was William de Castleford, who was also rector of St Pancras in Winchester. Castleford seems to have taken de Cloune as his model and absented himself from the Hospital. Accordingly, Wykeham had him excommunicated for non-residence, which also meant that he lost his rights to St Pancras as well.

There is room for a little confusion over what happened next. In the Bishop of Winchester's documents, there is a statement that de Cloune had given up his case, renounced his appeal, and had left the Hospital 'ownerless'. Clearly, Wykeham claimed here that de Cloune had resigned his office by the very fact of leaving the country. Next, it is stated that the Bishop collated Nicholas de Wykeham, clerk, as Master of the Hospital. However, when de Cloune died in 1382, Wykekam appointed his friend, John de Campeden as Master, although Nicholas was still alive. Campeden made a note alongside the statement that Nicholas had been collated, in which he said to the contrary, and very precisely, that Wykeham had kept the Hospital in his own administration for nine years, two weeks and five days, and that Nicholas had never been collated to the Mastership. From this, it would appear that, as in the case of Hyde (who, as a matter of coincidence was Vicar of 'Wykeham'), the whole of the Hospital property was sequestered to Nicholas, but that the bishop kept a firm hand on the tiller. de Cloune apparently retained the title, but none of the benefits or duties of Master until his death. It was only his death in September 1382 that enabled Wykeham to appoint a new Master. Again, the fact of a perpetual benefice seems to be highlighted.

Nicholas Wykeham was not exciting as Master, or whatever title is given to him. His time was spent in retrenchment, without which the Hospital would undoubtedly have failed. This does not lead to much apparent action, but it did provide the means and the platform from which the next Master could safely move forward. Wykeham's appointment of his friend, John de Campeden, as Nicholas' successor to run St Cross proved to be most fortunate for the Charity.

de Campeden had already had some slight dealings with St Cross. As canon of Southwell, he had been one of the witnesses of Stowell's renunciation. At the time of his appointment, he was rector of Cheriton and Archdeacon of Surrey. Although he was a great friend of Wykeham's, no chances were taken over the safety of the funds. de Campeden had to work within the framework of the bull *Quia Contingit* and annually produce an inventory and account of his work. Even de Campeden started *in absentia*. His induction was carried out by the Hospital Steward, Sir Henry de Derneford, in March 1383, not with Campeden but on his chosen representative. The report of the time reads: 'Sir Henry, the Steward, led William the procurator to the outer gate of the Close of the Hospital and by delivery of the ring of the same gate, inducted him into the corporal possession of the said Alms House or Hospital, with all its rights and appurtenances; and committed to him the care and administration of all its spiritual and temporal goods. Then leading him to the door of the church, he also gave and delivered the ring of such door.' Next came the bell ropes and a ring on the bells, and then a procession to the altar where Sir Henry delivered 'the cups, books, vestments and other ornaments of the said church of the same Hospital; and assigned him a stall in the choir'. They then crossed over to the hall 'to the place of the greatest honour, where the Master and the Chief Warden of the same Hospital were used to sit down; and made and monished all the brethren, clerks, and other servants and ministers of the same House, humbly to obey and deferentially to wait on, and serve with effect' the new Master.

Once actually in St Cross, de Campeden worked very hard for the Hospital. He was able to use funds and income which had been reclaimed by Nicholas Wykeham. His first care was for the brethren. The fact that he had 11 sets of rooms built to provide accommodation for 13 brethren seems strongly to support the fact that de Cloune did pull down brethren's quarters in order to make money from their materials. Perhaps, as 11 places were built for the 13 brethren, it may be assumed that two remained standing despite de Cloune's vandalism. The new homes were in the old place, to the south of the church. Thus, although the Master was now to the north of the church, near the Hundred Menne's Hall, and although the main Hall was also to the north, the centre of accommodation remained firmly to the south. This housing must have been at least adequate. The growing importance of St Cross under de Campeden led the Earl of Kent to choose the Master's Lodge as his home whilst in the city for the Winchester parliament in 1393.

Next, de Campeden turned his attentions to the church, which had also fallen into disrepair over the last 40 years. First, in 1384, he rebuilt the church tower, and roofed over the chancel and aisles. He then put in the eight glazed windows in the lantern, beneath the belfry, and inserted the 16 lights in the choir triforia, greatly improving the brightness of the church as well as helping with airing it. Stalls were erected in the body of the church, probably providing seating in there for the first time. The Lady Chapel was provided with benches and stalls for 13 brethren. On the south side, the chapel received the images of the Blessed Virgin Mary and St John the Baptist from the 'Solar of the porch chamber', inhabited by the Chaplain. A Purbeck marble altar was placed at the east end in 1385. Above the altar, de Campeden raised a tall reredos. The original altar slab, easily identified by its five consecration crosses, was rediscovered in the 19th century, and placed at the base of the altar at the east end of the church. In 1929, the slab was restored to its original position as the top of the table. The choir roof slope was slightly altered. The altar screens were removed and the central columns there changed into octagonal shapes, perhaps to replace the strength lost in removing the screen. Appearances would suggest that parts of the screens were then used to close off the choir from the aisles. The two lower windows of the east end were blocked. As mentioned earlier, in 1390 the whole church was tiled with encaustic tiles.

Outside, in the grounds of the Hospital, de Campeden made other improvements. He is recorded as having rebuilt the brewery 'on the side against the bank of the river', and installed in it a new and larger furnace. This description would place the brewery in the area which is normally regarded as being the Hundred Menne's Hall. He also repaired the gutter that ran through the building. There is no sign of this in either the building now accepted as the brewery or in the Hundred Menne's Hall. With the normal ration of beer provided in the constitutions, if the Hospital were full, then the new brewery would need a larger furnace than when the numbers had been allowed to fall. Much later, a diocesan licence was granted in 1782 to convert the Hundred Menne's Hall into a brewhouse, as the actual feeding of the hundred men no longer seemed to exist, because the Charity apparently provided money rather than food.

18   *The stone of John de Campeden, to be found in centre aisle. Note the form of the 4 in 1410, resembling half a figure eight.*

de Campeden's accounts for 1409 show that he brought stone from Southampton to pave 'the cloisters', had provided a new clock, and spent money on the vault. Food for his own household included meat, red and white herrings, lampreys, oil and salt. Everything was an earnest of de Campeden's intention to bring to the institution its proper prestige and ability to work to its highest level.

The total that de Campeden spent is recorded as £1,822—this despite the fact that he frequently complained that the income of the Hospital was really inadequate for normal expenses. This is almost certainly true, as accounts show that the whole income for 1390 was slightly over £269. A list of the staff in the Hospital in 1390 notes the Master, Steward, 13 brethren, eight clerks, a clerk of chambers, seven choristers, four chaplains, a deacon, a sacrist, an '*informator pueribus*', who presumably was a teacher employed at the school within the grounds, two valets, a barber, three bakers, three brewers, one cook, one gardener, two porters, three carters, plus eight horses and three carts. To employ all these people and to do this immense amount of work and spend so much money (certainly no less than £300,000 in 1994 equivalent), de Campeden himself must have been a splendid beggar and able to appeal to a vast number of moneyed lords and ladies. Any other answer involves assuming de Campeden to be a man of immense wealth himself, which contemporary records suggest was unlikely.

A detailed survey of 1401 gives the full value of the lands belonging to St Cross bordered by 'the great river running towards Twyford, and so into the sea, commonly called Ichen Streeme'. From this terrier, it appears that the two water mills, hinted at in 1392, were both working, and that there was an orchard of three and a half acres extent, to the north of the church, worth three shillings and sixpence yearly. The Porter's garden was valued at four pence per year. It is thus obvious that the grounds spread far beyond the area now walled in.

de Campeden died in 1410, having done a wonderful job for St Cross. It was once more well set for the future. He was buried in the church, appropriately before his new altar. His brass, marked with his sign manual, the emblems of Our Lord's passion, can now be found in the north transept. The same signs, not strictly his heraldic device, can also be seen in a shield on one of the bosses in the nave. It lies between the shields of two other vital figures in the history of St Cross—Wykeham and Beaufort. In the nave aisle, almost central between the last two pews before the choir, is to be found a small stone, easily missed, marked J D C and dated 1410 in the old medieval figures. This is the last memorial to de Campeden, and he would undoubtedly be pleased to think that worshippers passed over it on their way to his new altar some five hundred and eighty-five years later.

Chapter VI

New Foundation

Whilst de Campeden was still involved in his great work at St Cross, Cardinal Beaufort ascended the episcopal throne of Winchester. His interest in the Foundation became at once apparent on the death of the Master. To succeed de Campeden, he appointed one of his most trusted servants, John Forest. John was, like Beaufort, illegitimate, but, unlike Beaufort, of a comparatively humble family. After entering the Church, he had become a prebendary in Lincoln, and held the living of Middleton Stoney in Oxfordshire. As so many priests of the time were, he was an unashamed pluralist. Having found favour with Beaufort, whilst the latter was Bishop of Lincoln, he followed him south to Winchester. Here Forest became rector of Wonston, Master of the Hospital of Godshouse in Portsmouth, and Archdeacon of Surrey, apart from his duties at St Cross. In 1417, he was appointed Vicar-General to Beaufort, in which post he was responsible for the day-to-day management of the diocese. He was also Treasurer to Beaufort's household. Forest was so highly esteemed that the convent paid him a pension of 5 marks for his 'esteemed counsel and future goodwill'.

On appointment as Dean of Bath and Wells in 1425, he resigned the mastership of St Cross. Probably, he was too competent as a career churchman to do a good job at St Cross. What was needed after the tribulations of the previous 50 years and the hard, splendid work of de Campeden in the last almost thirty, was someone who put the Hospital first and foremost in his actions. Clearly, John Forest could not, and did not, do this. St Cross did not suffer as in the days of de Cloune, but it did not surge forward as it might have done as a consequence of the foundations laid by de Campeden.

During Forest's period as Master, the church was redecorated, apparently at Beaufort's insistence and probably at his expense, and it was thought that it should then also be re-dedicated. Beaufort was certainly present at the service in October 1420 and may well have officiated at it. A close link with the College is shown by the fact that, according to the annals of Winchester College, the Master gave a dinner in the College Hall, after the ceremony. The guests are listed as the Steward Fromond, Boreway, Kyngesylle, Pyes, Smythford, Tychfield, Welman, three people from St Cross, four singing men from St Cross, and (perhaps best of all) 'Deverose, the litigious tailor'. Smythford was a chaplain at St Cross and also a fellow of Winchester College.

After John Forest's promotion, came another Forest—Thomas. In his will, John made 'his kinsman', Thomas Forest, his chief executor, so there is no doubt that this is another example of 'family first'. Incidentally, John's will left £40 for Beaufort to buy himself a jewel, laid down that his own funeral expenses were to be no more than £20, and provided money for a thousand masses to be said for his soul. It would seem that he died a rich man, but could not be called arrogant.

Thomas was not the man that John had been. Although he was a bachelor of law, and held the benefices, amongst others, of North Stoneham and Alresford, he received no great church preferences—this despite the fact that he and his family had the support of Beaufort. Moreover, he was later accused of negligence and a total lack of action over John's will. His lack of business sense is perhaps illustrated by the fact that he died intestate. He does not seem to have been very active in St Cross, either. On the other hand, he did not despoil it. It merely chugged along gently under his mastership, which lasted from 1425 to 1463. It was in his time that the Beaufort foundation came to birth.

There is other evidence, apart from the appointment of John Forest, that Beaufort had his eye on the Hospital. In 1440, it was while he was staying at St Cross that he had a charter drawn up for Winchester College. Despite the many homes available to the Bishop of Winchester, he chose to come out to the Hospital, stay there, and transact important business there. 'The Brokage Books' of Southampton show that in late 1439 and again in early 1440 he was having large supplies of iron nails, tiles, and other building materials sent to Winchester. They appear to have been stockpiles for his projected foundation. When construction of the new buildings was well under way in 1444, the records show 1,000 nails and 200 tiles being sent from Southampton to St Cross. In the same period ale, wine, fish and fruit were all sent to the Hospital in quantities which suggest that they were to feed the workmen. Henry VI showed his support of Beaufort and for the almshouse by making an annual grant of a tun of Gascon red wine to the Master and brethren. He also agreed to make a royal grant of £500 yearly to the Almshouse, in return for a payment by Beaufort, made direct to the Treasury, of £8,900. Unfortunately, it was a grant that was never paid.

The sort of foundation that Beaufort had in mind would demand a considerable expenditure to build and maintain. As early as 1439, the Cardinal began buying lordships, manors and other properties to finance the scheme. In 1443, he was granted a licence

19 *Cardinal Beaufort from an effigy in Bishops Waltham.*

enabling him to pass the properties to anyone he wished, and a second licence to permit him to grant properties up to a value of £500 per annum to St Cross. Eventually, in 1446, he passed a number of investments to the Hospital —the manors of Henstridge and Charlton Camville in Somerset, Tarrant Launceston in Dorset, Amesbury, Winterbourne Earls and the borough of Wilton in Wiltshire, the fee-farm of Southampton, the advowsons of the churches of Crondal and St Faith (almost adjoining the Hospital), the free chapels of Ecchinswell and St James in Winchester, plus Cold Henley, and, finally, the income from the Hospital of St John at Fordingbridge. The last-named fitted very well with the early history of St Cross!

This impressive list fell far short of providing the Charity with the income of £500 Beaufort had postulated. Indeed, it would appear that the total annual income was valued in 1446 at less than £200. A year later, on Beaufort's death, the value is put at £158 13s. 4d. per year. Apparently, the Cardinal anticipated that his executors would somehow make up the shortfall from his estate. During the 19th-century lawsuit, the Attorney-General accepted a list of the property given by Beaufort to the almshouse. It differs slightly from the original of 1443, and contains the chapelries of Alderholt and Ecchinswell, the parsonages of Yately, Crondal and Long Sutton, the Hospital of St John, Fordingbridge, St Cross Mills, 10 small properties in St Faith, the churchyards of St Faith and St James, the rectory and demesne lands of St Faith, Cold Henley, fee farm from Southampton, the manors of Henstridge, Amesbury, Winterbourne Earls, Tarrant Launceston, and Owslebury, the town and borough of Wilton, and the vicarage of Crondal. Perhaps the few changes are extras provided by the executors. Charlton Camville is omitted. Perhaps it was at once sold in order to provide capital for building. Some changes are clearly merely legal niceties to ensure total description. In 1853, this list was quoted as having an annual value of £3,569 11s. 9d.—a far cry from the less than £200 four hundred years earlier. Unfortunately, by 1853 a large proportion of the lands and advowsons had long since passed away from the Charity.

Beaufort intended that his charity should be 'the Almshouse of Noble Poverty'. Somehow it has an even better ring in his Latin description—'*Domus Eleemosynaria Nobilis Paupertatis*' (even if part of the Latin is cribbed from the Greek). Thomas Forest, and each succeeding Master of the de Blois Foundation, was to control the new charity in tandem with the old. For this work, there was an extra £20 per year, which was to be paid out of the income from the manor of Henstridge, plus £20 'for livery'. The Cardinal's plan was that there were to be 35 brethren and three sisters. All were to be single, have fallen on hard times through accident or disability, and be either members of Beaufort's family or of gentle birth. In one sense, it was to be a haven for the 'civil servants' of the Lancastrian experiment, who were not of noble birth even if they were gentle-folk, had no lands to provide income, yet had served the country well. Spiritually, they would be ministered to by two chaplains, who were to be paid £8 per year, with an allowance of £20 'for livery', as with the Master. The brethren and sisters each were to receive £3 6s. 8d. annually 'from the Master's hands', making an assumption that he would always be present to do so. They were also to be given 10 shillings for their washing and shaving— the washing being that of their clothes and the shaving to be done by the barber. To differentiate them from the black-gowned members of the original Foundation, their

20   *The brethren's rooms built by Beaufort.*

cloaks were to be deep red, with a badge of a cardinal's hat worn on the chest. These garments were to be replaced annually and in 1451 the cost of making 38 cloaks is noted as 30s. Presumably this meant that there was a full complement of members of the Order in 1451. One of the duties of the new foundation as a group was to pray daily for the well-being of Henry VI, Queen Margaret and Cardinal Beaufort.

De Blois' original Foundation had provided for single cells for each occupant, on the lines of the leper hospitals upon which most residential charities were built. Because the people to be helped by the Beaufort scheme were not the normal recipients of charity, the houses provided were to be more on the lines of a college than of an almshouse. The rooms were set on three sides of St Cross church and to its north and west—not the traditional south. Unusually for charities, and even for some collegiate buildings, the apartments contained a large sitting room to the front, two small rooms to the back, plus a toilet. Four sets of rooms, two flats upstairs and two below, clustered round each staircase. Between each set there was a small lobby, so that all brethren had some degree of privacy. Major features of the architecture were the huge chimneys on the inside of the quadrangle, which led away the smoke from the fireplaces in each flat. The whole formed three sides of a square, joining the Great Hall with the church. The Hall itself was lit by three windows in each of the north and south walls, several of which carried Beaufort's arms and motto 'A Hono et Lyesse' (simply translated—to honour and joy).

Directly facing the church, from the northern side of the quadrangle, is the Beaufort Tower. The rooms in its three storeys could be approached either through what is now the hatch used by the Porter to give out the Wayfarers' Dole, or via the steps inside the Hall and at its east end, or by way of a doorway at the base of the structure's western tower, or finally through the upstairs of the present Porter's lodge. The main portion of the building was dedicated to rooms for the Master. The space beneath these rooms formed a gateway into the Hospital accommodation. On the western side of the ceiling of this space, opposite what is now the point at which the Wayfarers' Dole is given, but which was then a door into the Master's house, is a carving of a man's face, upside down. Legend has it that it represents de Cloune, and was placed upside down to show the contempt in which he was held. Its position was such that it was a daily reminder to successive Masters as they left their house not to act in the wicked style of de Cloune. The central boss in the archway is a carving of leaves formed into a cross and surrounded by a crown of thorns—a rather beautiful and unusual piece of stone work.

On the Beaufort Tower, looking towards the church, was a niche which was filled with a statue of the Virgin Mary and child. She was wearing the high crown associated with her. This has led to the occasional comment that the statue really represented the milkmaid of de Blois' foundation legend. On the other side of the gatehouse, there are three niches. Beaufort, dressed as a cardinal, kneeling in prayer and looking inward, still inhabits the western one. The other niches are now empty. However, it seems likely that Beaufort was turning in adoration towards the cross, as both the highest symbol of his faith and the badge of the Hospital of St Cross. He was proud enough and important enough not to have allowed himself to be shown as kneeling to anything less. This probably occupied the central niche. The eastern niche held perhaps either Henry de Blois or St John. Beaufort is known to have seen parallels between his life and that of de Blois. Both

The quadrangle showing, from the left, the brethren's rooms, the Hall, the Beaufort Tower and a small section the ambulatory.

Beaufort kneeling in a che at front of Beaufort wer, with the spaces which is probable held a cross and statue of Henry de Blois.

were of royal blood, both were papal legates and Bishops of Winchester for a lengthy
period. Each was extremely wealthy and important on the national and international
stages. Perhaps Beaufort became interested in St Cross because he was intrigued by its
connection with a man whom he saw as a sort of twin. The connection of the Charity
with St John is not one which would have had any personal appeal to him. There is
another pointer in the seal of Thomas Forest, now in the Public Records Office, with a
date of 1452. This shows Beaufort to the left, a crucifixion in the centre, and Henry de
Blois to the right. On balance, therefore, it is likely that the eastern empty niche was once
the home of a statue of Henry de Blois. Below these statues is a line of busts which are
normally said to be John of Gaunt, Henry V, Henry VI, Margaret of Anjou. There are a
number of other, quite reasonable claimants for the honour, but this set stresses Beaufort's
royal connections, as does his coat of arms, and so has a good chance of being correct.
The shields are the arms of the royal house and of Beaufort. A quite remarkable feature
of the building of all these structures is that they seem to have been completed by 1447,
though they were not started until 1444.

The names of a number of brethren of the Almshouse of Noble Poverty, but none
of sisters, have come down. John Turke had entered Winchester College in 1415 and been
a fellow from 1421 to 1424. A fellow Wykehamist was John Knight, who had been at the
College from 1419, and was a fellow from 1426 to 1441. John Smythford had entered the
College in 1409, had been present at the rededication of St Cross in 1420 and was
Chaplain to the Almshouse of Noble Poverty, certainly in 1451 if not before. The links
with the College remained firm. Others who were not Wykehamists, but whose names
have been preserved, are Henry Chambre, John Grenewyche, William Thomas, John
Browning, who was expelled for reasons not stated in 1454 and replaced by Richard
Deryck. When it was reported in 1449 of Henry Chambre that 'he has gone the way of
all flesh', he was replaced by Richard Morreys. A further group of replacements mentioned
are Robert Vaughan replacing Robert Brian in 1445, Thomas Lago taking over from
Richard Sheldrake in 1461, Robert Barton vice John Green in 1451, and William Thomas
appointed in 1487. Except for William Thomas in 1487, each is a replacement for a dead
brother. This suggests that the Order was kept up to numbers and men had to await dead
men's shoes before entry, at least until the 1460s. Of the chaplains, John Smythford and
John Gamelyn were together in the early 1450s. Walter Rede was appointed perpetual
Chaplain to the Order of Noble Poverty by Bishop Waynflete in 1458, in what was
perhaps a gesture of apology. Rede had been a member of the St John the Baptist Hospital
in Oxford when Waynflete closed it and transferred its possessions to his newly-founded
Magdalen College. Additionally to the appointment, in a special dispensation, Waynflete
permitted Walter not to be 'bound to attend at the Masses and other canonical Hours to
be solemnly celebrated in the choir of the Church of the Hospital'—a very considerable
concession. There is a brass in the choir robing room which commemorates William
Sandres, who died in 1464 whilst still a Chaplain of the new foundation.

Another interesting brass, because of its connection with Beaufort, is that of John
Newles:

> The yere of our Lord MCCCCL and two,
> Upon the xi day, in the month of Feverer
> The soul of John Newles the body passed fro'.

> A brother of this place, resting under this stone here,
> Born in Beaune, squyer and servant more yan xxx yere
> Unto Harry Beauford, Busshop and Cardinal.
> Whos soules God convey, and his moder dere,
> Unto the bliss of Heven that is eternel. Amen.

John still rests in peace, but his stone and brass now lie under the back pews of the church, with regular worshippers kneeling above him.

The accounts for St Cross in 1451 underline a crucial difference between the brethren of the old and new foundations. Whereas the original Charity catered specifically for those unable to look after themselves, payments in 1451 show the new brethren to have been active. Brother John Lydeford was paid his expenses for riding to London on business for the brethren. Brother John Bromley was paid for riding to Shaftesbury to transact some business with reference to 'Launston'. Another brother, John Skynner, was paid for three lambs he had sold. This shows the men to have been still looked upon as capable of transacting business as well as physically fit enough to ride fairly long distances.

These accounts also show that there must have been sisters amongst the members of the Almshouse of Noble Poverty, even if their names go unrecorded. John Sabale and two workers were paid for putting a new copper in the 'House of the Sisters'. John Wolford received 6s. 10d. for putting a beam into the wall for a pulley to raise the lid of the copper that had just been installed.

It is impossible to tie down any numbers or names for the sisters. Nevertheless, they have a special place in the story of St Cross. It is said that the eerie figure of a nun can at times be seen outside the tower which leads into what is assumed to be their living quarters. However easy it is to find a natural explanation of the phenomenon in the reflection of windows and the movement of trees, surely St Cross deserves at least the story of a ghost!

Little can be found about the life of the brethren. However, payments were made to Thomas Wells who was steward for all the mansions in Wiltshire, Dorset and Somerset. There were also two other stewards for the brethren in the Hospital. Robert Gooderegrome was butler to the new foundation. It also had its own cook, cook's servant and barber. The deduction from this little list must be that life could not have been too hard within St Cross walls.

The accounts have the quaint comment of a payment to 'Nicholas Hoy, the Undersheriff of Somerset and Dorset for obtaining his friendship'. A little bribery and corruption, perhaps—but very openly displayed! Bribery on a separate scale is maybe shown by the provision of a cygnet and six capons for the Bishop, plus a similar presentation to the Master. Clearly, the officers of the Almshouse of Noble Poverty would be well looked after, too.

Assuming the 38 cloaks each to have found a place upon a back, and adding the chaplains, cooks and other servants, plus the similar regiment headed by 13 brothers of the original foundation, St Cross must have housed about seventy people at that stage. All the evidence supports the traditional idea that the nun's quarters were on the east side of the quadrangle, opposite the brothers. An early 19th-century record comments that there had been damaged chimneys, similar to those on the west side of the square, existing along the ambulatory. Attempts to repair them had failed, and they had been pulled down in the 18th century, leaving the present lathe and plaster face. There is thus some slight evidence of provision of 'home fires' there. To this must be added the fact of the boiler paid for in 1451. Even so, there would still apparently be a shortfall in accommodation if the only places available were those that Beaufort had built. The inescapable conclusion must be that the dwellings to the south of the church were still in use, perhaps for the various servants. It would only be with the decay of the Almshouse of Noble Poverty that all could come to be concentrated in the quadrangle by the church.

With records of so many members of the new foundation still existing, it is quite clear that all started well. However, an unnamed Carthusian monk, who was Beaufort's confessor, warned him that he had heard stories of his officials at St Cross receiving gifts and bribes. Further reports in 1455 speak of unrest and unhappiness in St Cross. Perhaps the expulsion of Browning in 1454 was an augury of things to come.

From the very first, the Almshouse of Noble Poverty suffered from what in modern parlance is called a 'cash-flow problem'. Accounts produced in 1451 show a total expenditure of £307 14s. 5d., with a total income of £183 13s. 8d., leaving a deficit of £124 0s. 9d. As this was a by no means unusual feature of the accounts, none of which to that date really balanced, the problem was a growing one. Yet it was not the internal disciplinary problems, or the financial difficulties which were to prove the real ruin of Beaufort's Foundation, but legal and political considerations.

Quite legally, Beaufort had bought or received properties from the King. Unfortunately, the lands had been acquired by Beaufort personally and passed to the Master and brethren of his new Order, which was not set up as a corporate body. Hence, when debts arose, the Order could not sue in a court to gain redress. Nor was there a permanent line of succession to the properties, as the Master and brethren would die in due course. This would perhaps not have mattered if many of the lands acquired had not formerly belonged to the Montagu family, which was anxious to regain them. Whilst Beaufort was Lancastrian in the Wars of the Roses, the Montagus were Yorkist.

There were soon signs that the lands were under attack. So many grants had been made by Henry VI that the crown was short of money. In 1450, an Act of Resumption was passed, by which all lands formerly belonging to the crown but disposed of by Henry VI were to be taken back. However, St Cross did not suffer at this stage, as one section of the Act of Parliament specifically exempted all properties bought from the King by Beaufort and then granted to the Master and brethren of St Cross. Further 'any person or persons entred into the manors aforesaid by lawfull title of entre or recovered them by title of right or theire Auncestors whose heires thei bien or having restitution of their enheritaunce' were also exempted. In other words, St Cross lands and those who bought from St Cross or were freely given lands by the Hospital did not have to return them. This was very favourable treatment, as even some of Henry VI's favourite charities, such as Eton, were not exempted from resumptions. Clearly, the fact that it was necessary for these special provisions for St Cross to be built into an Act of Parliament shows that the charity was in some danger of losing its lands, either by law or force.

The growing power of the Yorkist faction in the 1450s led Thomas Forest to take action. Together with the Bishop, Thomas petitioned the King for a new scheme. As a result, Henry VI granted a licence to Waynflete to found (effectively, refound) a perpetual Hospital for men and women within St Cross, and to call it the Hospital or Almshouse of Noble Poverty. This foundation should be a proper corporate body. The Bishop was given the right to elect the Master, and draw up rules for the brethren and sisters. One of the chief duties of the residents was to be to pray for the soul of Cardinal Beaufort and (but only after his death) Henry VI. All Beaufort's grants were now passed to the new corporation. Most important, the executors were given the power to add further possessions to the value of £300 annually to the Charity, which would bring it up to the £500 envisaged by Beaufort. To ensure that there was little possibility of troubles such as those that had plagued the Hospital under de Cloune, the Duke of Somerset was named Patron and Protector 'for the preservation of the almshouse'. This protection was to prove a very weak reed indeed, as Somerset was killed in the Battle of St Albans just one month later.

Bishop Waynflete, another Lancastrian, now became the official protector of St Cross. As the Yorkist power increased, so did the influence of the Montagus. Alice Montagu had married into the Neville family, and her son was the great Richard, Earl of Warwick, better known as 'the kingmaker'. When Edward IV seized the throne in 1461, he gave Alice a licence 'to enter into all castles, lordships, manors and other possessions of Thomas Montagu, late earl of Salisbury'. She also obtained an Act which permitted her to regain all estates which had been held by her grandfather in the 14th century. This enabled the family to take away from St Cross important assets such as Amesbury, Charlton Camville, Henstridge and Winterbourne Earls. They then flexed their political muscles by simply taking Wilton, which at no time had belonged to their family.

When the Wars of the Roses ended, Henry Tudor ascended the throne as Henry VII. He was the son of Beaufort's great-niece, Margaret Beaufort. Waynflete thought that this might just presage a moment of support for the Almshouse of Noble Poverty, and he set about a refoundation of the Charity on 6 August 1486. By now, only seven properties remained in possession of the Order and they produced a mere £44 per annum. Although the building work was complete, and still is the glory of St Cross, the income certainly could not maintain the vast Charity Beaufort had intended. Waynflete arranged that the Master of St Cross, Richard Harward, should receive an extra £3 a year for looking after the Foundation, which was to consist merely of two brethren and a Chaplain. The Bishop called the Chaplain also a 'chantrist', a not entirely unusual title, but a pleasant link to the present in view of St Cross's high musical tradition. As he was solely responsible for the Beaufort brethren, and was not part of the de Blois Foundation, the Chaplain was to receive £6 13s. 4d. per annum, whilst each of the brethren had a pension of £3 6s. 8d. Waynflete's sad comment on the loss of land was that 'time and the insatiable malice of man and by the craft of succeeding persons, the lordships, rents, tenements and possessions are wholly taken from the said almshouse and are occupied by the power of noble persons'. The Almshouse of Noble Poverty struggled on for perhaps two years in that attenuated form, but was soon merged totally into St Cross and disappeared from sight. It was not until 1881 that the distinctive deep red uniforms of the Order were once more seen.

There were only four Masters of the Almshouse of Noble Poverty in its short existence during the 15th century. Thomas Forest remained in charge until his death in 1463. He was succeeded by Thomas Chaundler, a Doctor of Divinity and a well known scholar. Before coming to St Cross, he had been a fellow of New College, then Warden of Winchester. He left St Cross in 1465 when he accepted the post of Warden of New College, Oxford. Other posts that he held were chancellor and prebendary of York, chancellor and prebendary of Wells, Dean of the Chapel Royal, and Dean of Hereford. Another learned gentleman followed. William Westbury remained at St Cross until 1473, when he became Provost of Eton. The last of the four was Richard Harward, who was an LL.D. He resigned in 1489, 'on condition that provision and chambers be assigned to him and to three of his servants'. This was agreed, and Harward remains the only Master to have also been a brother of St Cross. The Almshouse of Noble Poverty having died a

23   *The fire precautions!*

death, he was presumably regarded as one of de Blois' Foundation. His three servants were counted as being general to the whole Hospital. He died in 1493 and is buried in the church, though the exact spot has been lost since his brass was removed to the north transept. He must have been proud of his LL.D as he is shown wearing his doctor's cap. Alongside him is the impressive brass of de Campeden. Another brass in the north transept is to Thomas Lawne, rector of Mottisfont, although his precise connection with the Hospital was not clear. de Campeden and Lawne are both buried in the chancel, and it is probable that Harward was buried there also.

St Cross claims certain 'relics' of Beaufort. In the kitchen are what are called his salt cellars, candlesticks and leather jacks. Whilst all are of the right period, it is extremely unlikely that any was owned or used by the cardinal. In the Lady Chapel, there is what is named 'Beaufort's chair'. It is still in use. Whenever a new brother is installed in either the de Blois' Foundation or the Almshouse of Noble Poverty, the Master sits in the chair to receive the postulant into the brotherhood. Sadly, it has to be said that it was probably made no less than sixty years after the death of Beaufort himself.

An idea of the casual attitude to the possibility of fire damage, despite the amount

24 *One of the fire buckets. Note how the small crosses have been moved to outside the Cross Potent.*

of wood in the buildings, open fires in each of the brethren's homes and an open, virtually unprotected, fire in the Hall, was the fact that not until the late 1400s were any fire precautions provided: and then the total was only six leather buckets hanging in the hall.

A sign of St Cross's importance is to be found in the centre of the city of Winchester. The Butter Cross there was in fact provided for the city by the Hospital, and is noted as having been given by the Fraternity of the Holy Cross—the brethren of St Cross, not the similarly named separate organisation founded by Henry VI. At the time of its presentation it was the City Cross, the centre of a busy area. Around it were the city pump, stocks, pillory and cage, and on either side were the prettily named buildings of Heaven and Hell. It is often attributed to Cardinal Beaufort, as it was he who organised all the dealings in the matter. The present cross is a modern replacement.

CHAPTER *VII*

A Visitation

For three years, John Lychefield, another LL.D, presided over the affairs of St Cross. At his death in 1492, the Bishop appointed Robert Sherborne as Master. He is probably the most visible Master of them all. His motto 'Dilexi Sapientam' (I have loved wisdom) and his initials, R.S., are to be found carved on walls and in windows in several places about the Hospital.

Robert Sherborne was a Wykehamist who early attracted the attention of both Church and state by his ability. At various times he was used with success on special services by Henry VII. Whilst at St Cross, he was also canon of Lincoln Cathedral, archdeacon of Taunton, archdeacon of Nottingham, prebendary of Wells, and Dean of St Paul's. He actually became Bishop of St David's in 1505, but did not give up his post in the Hospital until 1508, when he became Bishop of Chichester.

One of his carvings of initial and motto is to be found in the present kitchen of the Porter's lodge. It is dated 1503 in the style of 15th-century arabic numerals, and stretches all across the fire mantel from side to side. From this it may be deduced that, although the date is well after the building of the Beaufort Tower, which included accommodation for the Master, Sherborne may have preferred to remain in the old house.

In the window of the passage outside the Hall, leading to the kitchen, there is a glass which reads 'Dilexi S.pam'. 'S.pam' is obviously an abbreviation for *sapientam*. There are also two pieces of glass which are used simply to fill space. One reads 'R.S.' and the other has the date of 1497 in Arabic numerals of the same period of those in the Porter's lodge. The building of the new kitchen is often attributed to the Beaufort era. However, these initials in the glass do suggest that Sherborne was at least involved in some portion of the work. The splendid fireplace in the kitchen dates back to the 15th century, but could relate to either Sherborne or Beaufort. If the whole of the area from the Porter's lodge, through the Beaufort Tower, and into the Hall was dedicated to the Master, he certainly had a very large space for one man. This makes a splendid contrast to the tiny cell provided for the Chaplain in the early days.

Sherborne's initials and motto are to be found carved in the ambulatory and outside on the pillar below the oriel window in the centre of it. In fact, the stonework is a modern replacement, and has the date 1939 carved in the pillar at the back. However, this portion of St Cross was certainly at least re-shaped in Sherborne's time, and gives the appearance now of being almost totally 16th-century in design and style. On the lower floor, the ambulatory leads to what was once a door into the north transept of the church, so that Masters could move both dry-shod and unnoticed from home to work. Manuscripts suggest that the first Master to join church and home was John de Campeden, although nothing remains now that can be specifically identified as coming from his time. Upstairs, at the end of the long infirmary, was a window which enabled the sick to look down at the church and to hear its services. Facing them, covering the south wall, was a wall painting of the crucifixion. Both window and door are said to be the work of Sherborne's time, although the window, from what can now be seen of it, would appear to be earlier. Each is now blocked by the central heating boiler and machinery.

The probability is that all these areas benefited in some degree from repair work under Sherborne. In consequence, as the work was being done, he ensured that his mark was clearly visible—a common practice amongst builders of his time. He might well be regarded as having completed the work started on Beaufort's orders.

St Cross lay within the parish of St Faith, and reports of the late 1400s talk of the deterioration of the church of St Faith because of 'the decay in people'—presumably meaning a fall in population. Eventually, it became clear that neither the rector, who would normally be expected to shoulder the burden, nor the parishioners could afford to maintain the church. They approached the Hospital of St Cross to obtain permission to worship there. St Cross was not an 'open' church, being more in the style of a collegiate chapel,

25 *Ambulatory from the outside.*

and permission was needed before outsiders could regularly worship there. Consent was swiftly granted. Now that the parishioners had a new place of worship, they wished to desert their old building completely, and in 1507 received a licence to pull down St Faith's. All that is now left to suggest a church of the past is the cemetery at the corner of Kingsgate and St Cross Road. In the official documents, the parish is described as consisting of about 900 acres, 'of which 670 arable, 200 downland and 30 pasture and water meadow'. Since 1507, the parishioners have used St Cross as their parish church, and the parish is now officially named St Cross with St Faith. Cardinal Beaufort had in fact given St Faith's to St Cross when founding his Almshouse of Noble Poverty, and it had become normal for the Master also to be rector of St Faith from 1446. However, the actual position of the parishioners from that date must be regarded as that of welcome guests.

The non-parochial status of St Cross in the 15th century is evidenced in the finances, as well as in the constant statement that it was without cure of souls. A regular custom in the Church in England was that there should be four gift days when all collections went to the rector or vicar. Bishop Asserio laid down as a diocesan law for Winchester that the four occasions should be Christmas, Easter, All Souls' Day, and the patronal festival of the church. His nephew, whilst Master, never received these oblations, and the accounts show that this was the case throughout the history of St Cross. This may at least have encouraged various spoilers to take what they could, when that which was regarded throughout the church as a legitimate addition to the stipend could not come to them. It was customary in general ecclesiastical usage for the chief parishioners to provide the bread and wine for communion, and for the congregation to take responsibility for the choir. There are any number of accounts in a variety of parish churches throughout England that bear witness to this. As late as 1526, in the Master's accounts for that time, after St Faith had, as it were, been merged into St Cross, the opposite is shown. John Rodford, Master of the choristers, received 10s. 9d. repayment of his expenditure, but the total provided for 'divers other necessaries bought for the exhibition of the choristers' came to 106s. 10d. There would seem to have been quite a considerable choir in the church. The amount is actually about ten shillings more than the money spent on buying bread and wine for 'Divine Service'. Both these expenses were met from the general receipts and endowments of the Hospital. Presumably the parishioners of St Faith were not against this saving of their own cash!

Until the villagers joined St Cross church, it had had no call for a font, for the inhabitants were all old men or nuns, and ecclesiastical law made it plain that fonts were the exclusive privileges of parochial churches. Now there was the possibility of babies from the parish, and the font from St Faith's was brought in and placed near the west door of St Cross. It fitted in well, as the basin is Norman or Early English in style, although the stand is of a later date. It is what is colloquially called 'a witches' font'. In the early days, it was believed deeply and sincerely that witches eagerly sought Holy Water to improve the efficacy of their spells. After a baptism, even though the font had been most carefully wiped dry, there might remain some vestiges of water that had been blessed. To prevent witches obtaining it, churches placed a locked cover over the top of the stone basin. Careful examination of the St Cross with St Faith font will show a repair on either side of the top of the basin where the hinge and lock had been placed to foil the witches. Hence—witches' font. Later, the font was moved to a new position in the north aisle.

Another migrant was the bell, brought in to grace the tower. The stone screens under the arches at the east end of the church are also from St Faith's, probably dating from the 15th century. Next to them are some plainer ones which were almost certainly in place before the new imports, and are of the 1200s. Their duty seems to be that of forming parcloses to the chancel.

There is a persistent legend that St Faith's church burnt down in 1509. Certainly this is untrue. A possible explanation may lie in the fact that church law demanded that anything that had been consecrated must not be left so that it might possibly be used by unhallowed hands. Hence, as the church was demolished, some things, like the screen, were transferred to other churches. However, there may well have been much left over, up to the completion of the demolition in 1509, when a huge fire might have been used to burn up what could not be used. This conflagration could easily have passed into local lore as the fire of St Faith's.

Above the brothers' stalls, there are wooden screens with medallions representing kings, queens and bishops, though it is uncertain which are which. Formerly, these medallions were described as representing biblical figures, though an examination of them makes that seem unlikely. Much of the carving is in the style of the 15th century, but the presence of the pelican of Fox confirms a date of early 16th century. One fanciful derivation for them is that they came from Wolvesey in the reign of Henry VIII. One of the medallions is claimed as Anne Boleyn, and when the bishop found her 'on show' after her execution, with Henry VIII due to visit shortly, he ordered the screens out of his palace. 'Waste not want not' being a good motto for a charity, St Cross accepted them and placed them above the brothers' stalls.

Unique in the furnishings is the lectern. It was carved in a period from about 1400 to about 1500, probably somewhere in the middle of the century. On its head it has a heart, which signifies the love of Christ above all and for us all. Its head is that of a parrot,

26 *Medallions of 'Kings, bishops and queens' above the brethren's stalls in the choir. The third from the right is traditionally held to be Anne Boleyn. Note Fox's pelican in the first medallion.*

with the nut-crushing beak, telling us that we merely repeat God's word parrot fashion. Eagles' wings uphold the word of God, showing that it can fly to the greatest of heights. The feet are webbed because God holds the waters in his hands, whilst the feet themselves clutch the orb of the world, emphasising that God holds the world safely. Nowhere else is there to be found such a mixture of a bird. To date, it has proved impossible to link it with any particular carver or school of woodworkers. Just possibly, then, it is the work of a local man. Its very uniqueness adds to this possibility, but does not prove it.

When Sherborne resigned, Bishop Fox appointed John Claymund to succeed him. He was a Lincolnshire man, who had been educated at Magdalen College School, and became successively a scholar, fellow and President of Magdalen College, Oxford. Whilst at Oxford, he obtained a prebendal stall at Wells, just at the time that Fox was beginning his episcopacy there. The two men found that they had much in common, and when Fox moved on to Winchester, Claymund was pleased to follow him into the post of Master at St Cross.

Soon the Bishop found the company of the Master and the surroundings of St Cross so much to his liking that he was spending a fair amount of time there, climbing up the stone steps at the east end of the hall into the Master's lodgings above. As he grew older, Fox became more and more frail—indeed he was blind and almost deaf by the time he died. To help him mount the stairs, a wooden handrail was added. It is of very rough craftsmanship, and gives the appearance almost as if someone had suddenly realised that Fox was due to visit that afternoon and would not be able to climb the stairs unaided—so swiftly a workman knocked this rail roughly together. Fox's pelican, almost worn away, stands on the lower post. Because of his liking for St Cross, the Bishop is said to have asked that, if he died there, he might be buried there. His symbol of a pelican plus the arms of the Bishop of Winchester are to be found on the end of an old pew in the north chancel. He died at Wolvesey and lies in his chantry, which he had prepared before his death, in Winchester Cathedral. In the past, the stair rail has been attributed to Sherborne's time. However, Sherborne became Bishop of St David's in 1505, whilst Fox only became Bishop of Winchester in 1501. There is no clear evidence of a close connection between the two men, a connection which is certain in Claymund's time. On balance, therefore, it seems most likely that the rail originates from the later period. The style is so rough that no stylistic inferences can be drawn.

When Fox founded Corpus Christi College, Oxford, his admiration for Claymund took a practical form. Claymund's past showed him to be a scholar, and his work as president of Magdalen College proved him to be an administrator. Fox, therefore, appointed him to be the founding President of Corpus Christi. As a result, Claymund had the constitutions of the College read for the first time, in the presence of many Winchester notables, including the Bishop, at the Hospital. He then resigned office as president of Magdalen, but retained St Cross until 1524 whilst also president of Corpus Christi.

Another scholar followed Claymund. John Innocent went up first to Cambridge for one year, then (no doubt recognising his error!) for four years to Oxford, where he became Bachelor of Law and a fellow of All Souls. Not until 1512 did he become a priest and from that date remained Fox's business administrator and chancellor, continuing in office under Gardiner. He became President of the Brotherhood of St John. Fox rewarded Innocent by collating him to the mastership of St Cross, to which he later added the deanery of St Paul's, and the mastership of Godshouse, Portsmouth, following in the earlier footsteps of John Forest. Fox and Innocent obviously had many occasions to work together.

Innocent's arms are a play upon his name. Heraldically, they are 'argent on a bend gules, a fair and Innocent virgin, stark naked, with hair loose about her shoulders, Or, her right hand holding two roses, and reaching over her head, and her left extended before her person.'

As Master, he carefully maintained his accounts through his Steward, William Pare. The details for 1526 have an interesting entry of 12d. given to the parishioners of Twyford 'in a reward for coming with banners at the Feast of Whitsuntide last'. The old quarrel over hay tithes was clearly now long forgotten. Other details give a clear idea of the life at St Cross. There is money for five dozen sheep 'killed (and expended)' for the men, which gave rise to 200 pounds of fat, not melted, which appears later in accounts for making lights. Thomas Whitmore, John Lambert, John Goodryke, William Lyster, Thomas Crokett, Richard Paynne, George Hurlock, John Rodford, Richard Hubank, Robert Bayly, John Crondall, Ralph Whetell, John Kynge, William Chamber, and William Pare himself are listed as Chaplains and Clerks, receiving between them £35 4s. in stipends and £116 4s. for their liveries. The brethren are named as William Sysson, Thomas Lucas, Gerard Arnold, Henry Elam, William Morris, Nicholas Everatt, William Cocks, Richard Treve, Richard Goode, William Barber, John Cherry, receiving £7 3s. in wages and 97s. 2d. for liveries between them. The servants are named as John Hill, Edward Knyght, Nicholas Coke, Charles Tenent, the common barber, the common laundress, the washer of vestments, and Peter Smith, at a total yearly cost of £8 5s. 10d. Eight servants, 15 clerks and chaplains to 11 brethren! Apparently money was given to the Hundred Hall Poor on Mondays, Tuesdays and Saturdays, plus some Feast Days, which cost the Hospital £7 8s. 8d. Additionally, the Master ordered 65s. to be spent on improving the brown and black bread distributed every Sunday, Tuesday and Thursday. Wheat, malt, sheep, salt fish, white herrings, pigs, geese, butter, fresh water and sea fish, eggs, mushrooms, 'divers kinds of wine', spices, figs all appear as items for the table. This is intended to represent the diet of the brethren, for there are separate and similar purchases bought 'for the proper use of the Inn of the Master of the house'. Two hundred pounds of iron were bought for making a clock—quite a weighty one at that! 'Fifteen ells of canvas' were purchased to make towels (!) for the Hospital. Two yards of green cloth were needed for the table in the Master's study. An interesting item is food bought for the gulls, though why this should be needed is not explained. Blood letting, presumably of sick brothers, cost 14d. Moles were apparently a problem in the grounds, and 'a certain man' was paid 12d. for catching them. Materials for sundry repairs, including two locks for the Master's house (had there been a break-in?) cost £28 13s. 10d. The dovecote must still have existed, as 3s. 4d. is received in rent for it during part of the year, this being reduced because the 'pigeons thereof were expended within the House'. There is much more in the same vein. If the accounts are to be the only guide, then St Cross and its inhabitants were well catered for.

It was a time of great religious and political turmoil. The Reformation philosophies were rapidly gaining ground. Cranmer, the Archbishop of Canterbury, was actually married though obviously a priest. Henry VIII wished to be free of all foreign control, such as that of the Pope, and he needed money. Attacking the Church might well solve both problems. He also wished to have his first marriage annulled so that he could marry Anne Boleyn. This so-called divorce question became the excuse he used to gain a measure of control over the Church in England, and to institute wide ranging reforms within it.

Thomas Cromwell was the chief instrument in effecting the policy. In theory he was aiming to reform the religious houses, but the 'hidden agenda' was that of closing as many as possible and seizing their endowments. He obtained a commission empowering him to hold a general visitation, over the heads of the diocesan bishops, in 1535. St Cross was too wealthy to escape this net.

Dr. Legh was sent to the Hospital on 20 September in that year in order to make a full visitation. Normally, a visitation by him was merely the prelude to closure. Legh was described in his own time as being a 'conceited young don whose arrogance was expressed offensively in his satraplike countenance'. Later, he became a master in Chancery and was knighted. Neither he nor Thomas Cromwell had any feelings of kindness towards the priesthood. Legh was known to be antagonistic towards ancient foundations. Finally, he was searching for money for his royal master. It was certain, then, that St Cross was in for a thorough examination.

Innocent and Pare had their books all in order. First they attempted to avoid visitation completely, because St Cross was not a religious house within the meaning of the commission. It was pointed out to them that this was a general visitation, and so included every type of religious establishment. Innocent explained that this was a benefice without cure of souls and so might perhaps not even be a religious house. Legh parried with the fact that St Faith was attached to it. Next, the Master argued that this was in no wise a monastic establishment and so could not be closed as one of the smaller residential houses. Legh agreed that this was so—either because his legal training made it clear that St Cross was exempt, or perhaps, as Hospital legend has it, he was suitably bribed. He did carry out a full visitation, and his rather mild report suggested that there were some matters which needed reformation.

> Poor men (by which he meant the brothers who lived in) shall have sufficient and proper clothing and food within the said House, according to the will of the Founder, and that it be not given to them in money counted in any manner for the same. Also that the hundred-hall-poor shall not be served as mendicants, like as was not long ago accustomed to be done; and such dinners shall be distributed to them who study and labour with all their strength at handiwork to obtain food: and, in no case, shall such alms be afforded to strong, robust, and indolent mendicants, like so many that wander about such places, who ought rather to be driven away with staves, as drones and useless burdens upon earth. And also, some discreet and honest priest of the House shall hear and teach the poor inhabitants here the Lord's Prayer, and the Apostles' Creed in English; which prayer and creed all the poor men shall say together in the Church before dinner. And also the Master, or President, shall not exhibit reliques, images, or miracles, when sought for; but shall earnestly exhort pilgrims and guests to give to the poor and needy what they would have offered for such purposes. And also the Master shall in nowise diminish the number of priests, presbyters, sacrists, and others within this House, that have been used to minister here, on the Foundation, or by custom; and he shall observe all and singular other things unbroken which the Foundation

aforesaid, or laudable custom, have hitherto required to be done here. Also, he shall have in this House a library; in which besides other necessary books, shall be placed printed volumes of the New and Old Testaments, the works of Jerome, Augustine, Theophylact, and others of the most ancient fathers of a similar kind.

Presumably this clause, listing the books to be held, did not entirely meet with Innocent's approval, as it is partially crossed out in the original document. Maybe some of the authors may have seemed to be too extreme for him. There is no evidence of the particular books ever having been placed in the library, although, having escaped closure when others had fallen, there would doubtless be a leaning towards doing what one was told and not attracting attention from the authorities. Certainly, the current Brothers' library has very little resemblance to that laid down! Innocent and Pare were told to produce to Thomas Cromwell, by Christmas 1535, 'all charters whatsoever of the first, second and third foundation, appropriations, bulls, privileges, and all popish muniments whatsoever' plus an inventory of all goods and chattels in the ownership of the Hospital, and a full rental list of all its property. As the Hospital remained open, and the charters were returned, it is clear that Cromwell could find no fault in them. Mention of three foundations would suggest that Legh was talking about de Blois, Beaufort, and Waynflete's efforts. At no time does he differentiate between the two types of brethren, nor does he actually ever mention Beaufort's or Waynflete's foundation by name. One last injunction was laid on the Master and brethren. They were to have a Mass within a month for the souls of the Founder, Henry VIII, and Queen Anne. Poor Anne! The prayers did not help her much, as she was executed the following May.

It is interesting to notice the orders about not showing off relics, or claiming miracles, and getting payment from pilgrims for such displays. There is no record in any of the St Cross documents of what these relics or pretended miracles might be—yet Legh must have felt that there was sufficient evidence of St Cross beginning to become a centre of pilgrimage for him to have made a special mention of it in his injunctions. Where money was received for seeing relics, it most often stayed in the hands of the exhibitor. Legh was doing his best to ensure that the poor benefited from all money that came to the Charity. How splendid, too, to read that the injunction to teach in English comes in the Latin phrase 'in idiomate communi', although practically every other word is in English!

Problems for the future were laid up with the phrase 'sufficient and proper food and clothing'. There was no definition of proper and it was left to future Masters to make their own gloss upon the word. However, Legh must have known how de Cloune had robbed the Hospital and deprived its inmates of a home, as can be seen by the orders not to reduce numbers in any way. Significant is the instruction that there must be no money equivalent for food and clothing. Despite the great wealth he had inherited, Henry VIII was being forced to borrow money from European bankers. He also debased the coinage, so that the same amount of gold made more coins than previously. The result of all this was that money payments would mean that the poor actually received less value than intended by the founders. Already, Pare's accounts suggested that there was a move in this direction. The strictures against sturdy beggars echo the law of the land. In 1536, it was enacted that 'impotent beggars' must receive a licence from their local J.P.'s to enable them to beg. 'Lusty beggars' were to be whipped at the cart tail and sent to their home parish, and have part of an ear cut off for a second offence. Six years later, parliament is complaining that some J.P.'s 'hath bene very remysse and negligent' in carrying out the Act. Legh was making sure that St Cross was not to be labelled thus. On the whole, the visitation certainly did no harm to the Hospital, and may well have done good by reminding people that it was there for a specific purpose.

The parish of St Faith was also brought into the visitation, but the only comment which seems to have been made is that the Master paid for four priests to minister to parishioners. The mere fact of it being mentioned may suggest that Legh at one time tried to make the multiplicity of priests into a reason for closure. That there were four priests officially attached to St Faith is borne out by accounts of a later date in 1541, when payments were still being made to four men.

Innocent must have been a much relieved man to see the back of the feared inspector, and to know that St Cross would continue as before. Apart from his successful emergence from the visitation—and a very big success it was—Innocent has left no mark on the Hospital. He may even be said to have left a negative impression behind him, for it was in his period that the rood loft was taken down. Cut down is a better description, as it was simply sawed away where it stood. For some years, the last few inches of wood stuck out from the wall as a mute reminder of the destructive power of the Reformation.

27   *Beaufort Tower.*

There is a small irony in Innocent's successful opposition to Legh. He himself became one of Thomas Cromwell's commissioners, inspecting the smaller religious houses with the intention of dissolving them. He must have learned from his own experience, and become good at the job, as there is a note in Cromwell's hand which says 'I must do something for Innocent'.

His successor in 1545, William Meadow (a prebendary of Winchester Cathedral), at once clashed with him. Whilst Innocent was Master, he bought five tenements in Sparkford from Robert Sherborne to endow his school in Berkhamsted. Meadow challenged his right to buy and give away these buildings, claiming that they belonged to the Hospital. The matter went to court and was decided in favour of Meadow. Perhaps momentary fame may be said to have come to him when he received a royal visit. When Philip was on his way from Southampton to Winchester in July 1554, prior to his marriage to Mary, there was a sudden downpour of rain. As he was riding and did not wish to ruin his clothes, he stopped at St Cross and spent the night there, as many pilgrims on their way to Canterbury had done before him. There is no record of where he slept, so no notices on the bed 'Prince Philip of Spain slept here', but it is virtually certain that he lodged in the Master's house in one of the rooms of the Beaufort Tower. Only these would have been big enough to provide shelter for the prince and his retinue, whilst also having limited access which could fairly easily be guarded. A very short Mastership followed Meadow. John Leffe was collated in June 1557, but died in August 1557. He was Vicar-General and keeper of spiritualities to Archbishop Warham, whose arms now appear in the Master's Office in consequence.

CHAPTER *VIII*

Trials and Tribulations

T he last Roman Catholic Bishop of Winchester was John White. He is best known for telling the congregation at Queen Mary's funeral that they should obey Queen Elizabeth, using the words 'For better is a living dog than a dead lion'. Speaking of religion, he had called on the congregation to resist the wolf of heresy if they saw it entering the fold. He even harked back to Trajan's comment that Romans should use the sword of justice to support him if he ruled justly, but against him if he ruled unjustly. This rash turn of phrase cost him a period in The Tower, though he died at South Warnborough, and was buried quietly in Winchester Cathedral.

If White's words were unwise, his choice of the last Catholic Master of Hospital was equally poor. He nominated Robert Raynolds, his Vicar-General, in August 1557. High up in the north-west window of the clerestory at St Cross is a pair of shields. The one to the left is that of White, surrounded, as of right, with the Garter. Next to it is a shield in which the arms of St Cross impale the arms of Winchester Diocese, also fully enclosed within the Garter. Obviously, this cannot be White's, nor would Raynolds be entitled to the Garter. It is probably meant to refer to Raynolds' dual rôle as Vicar-General to the Bishop and Master at St Cross, though the diocese is set, heraldically speaking, on the wrong side of the shield, perhaps because it was thought of as being seen from outside. It is noticeable that a number of Vicars-General to the bishop also held office at St Cross. Perhaps, having the ear of the bishop on an almost daily basis, they were able to ensure that they obtained this prized preferment. Incidentally, in the long history of Masters of St Cross, eight became bishops, eight were presented by the monarch in *commendam*, and four were chosen as the archbishop's option. This clearly underlines the national and clerical importance of the post.

Raynolds' appointment was a source of great trouble to St Cross. The Master held the same views as men like de Cloune. He was soon selling the Hospital's wheat and malt in the open market; but this was not sufficient for his ambitions. Using the St Cross seal, which was in his possession, he sold the mansion of Ashton. This had been in St Cross' possession for more than four hundred years, as it was one of the original endowments of the 1130s. Secretly, he did a deal with 'a certain Ralph Cleverly' by which the Hospital's 'Mansion House', the bakehouse, brewhouse, orchards and gardens were leased to him at a beneficial rate, in return for clandestine payments to the Master individually. There is almost cause for admiration at Raynolds' bare-faced swindling. Luckily for the Hospital, he was not destined to last long in office, for in 1559 he was forced to resign. It would be pleasant to say that his crimes had caught up with him, but it would appear that he was ejected as much as an extreme Roman Catholic as a robber.

Raynolds' successor was John Watson. Originally he had studied medicine, which he practised with success until he took Holy Orders. After being collated as Master of St Cross, he became successively prebendary and Dean of Winchester Cathedral, holding these in turn as a pluralist with the post of Master at the Hospital. When he was told that Queen Elizabeth was going to appoint him as Bishop of Winchester, he offered the Earl of Leicester £200 to persuade her not to do so. All in vain, for he was promoted in 1580, but was given special royal dispensation to remain as Master of St Cross also.

There is a story that Dr. Watson was chosen as a name for Sherlock Holmes' companion by Conan Doyle as a result of a visit to St Cross and the Cathedral. At any rate, the Sherlock Holmes Society made a special pilgrimage to the Hospital in 1991 to see at first hand the haunts of the original doctor and to study his signature. Graffiti is not a new failing. On the north-eastern red-brothers' stall there are the signatures of John Watson, 'Master of this place', Sir John Watson, Chanter, and Sir Henry Watson, Steward, all from 1572. It would seem that family favourites was also played at that time. Other men whose graffiti on the stalls still exist were Sir John Wrighte, curate and R. Ganet, singing man. What is interesting is the existence of a 'Chanter' and a 'singing man'. This was a period when the singing of masses and other services was being discouraged, yet St Cross still clearly followed the old line of song. Probably it was able to do so because of its uniquely independent status. Clearly, doodling whilst in church was quite an industry. On that same stall is a splendid little cameo of a highwayman holding up a coach.

28   *Stage coach hold-up graffiti carved into brethren's stall on north side of choir.*

Watson would have benefited from a legal training rather than courses in medicine and theology. Henry VIII had taken the first fruits and tenths payments from the Pope to the crown. Mary had restored them to Rome, but Elizabeth had taken them back again. The Hospital claimed that it did not have to pay these charges. Under Mary, the situation was clear as the Pope had removed the charge from St Cross. Now, Elizabeth's financiers were saying that English law made the Charity liable. Watson claimed that the statute relied upon actually exempted from payment all places that were 'founded and used, and the possessions thereof are employed for the relief of the poor'. Remembering the work of Raynolds, and probably aware of how other Masters had treated the funds, the Court of Exchequer demanded that the Bishop of Winchester should search his records to see whether this exemption might safely be claimed. Could it be said that the funds were used for the relief of the poor when the Masters were notorious for having sold goods belonging to the Hospital and kept the proceeds?

After a long search, the Bishop certified that the exemption could be claimed and went on to say categorically: 'And we found that the said house or hospital, at the time of the making of the Act of Parliament recited in the writ, and long before, was founded and used, and the possessions thereof had been employed, in the relief of the poor, and that now the said house or hospital is used and founded, and the possessions thereof employed, for the relief of the poor'. This judgement by the Bishop made it crystal clear that he did not consider that any resources of St Cross should be used by the Master for his personal gain.

All this took three years in and out of court, but ended with the Charity being exempted from payment of first fruits and tenths. 'It was adjudged by the same Barons (of the Exchequer) that the aforesaid warden or master of the hospital or house aforesaid, and the aforesaid house or hospital of the Holy Cross, without the walls of the City of Winchester aforesaid, be discharged from the first fruits and tenths aforesaid, from the time of making the Act of Parliament.' This, however, did notice the position of the Master in receiving and paying money. He was personally excused the duty of payment of dues, though he might still receive cash!

Watson also took on the law in attempting to have the leases granted by Raynolds annulled. It was a long and hard struggle. Eventually, however, after 'divers great and troublesome suits in law, to the great travail and expense of John Watson, clerk, now Master of the said Hospital', an Act of Parliament was passed in 1567. All the leases to Ralph Cleverly were overturned. It was also enacted that no premises or land within the precincts of St Cross or in the parish of St Faith could ever again be leased away from the Hospital and that no leases for lives were to be granted by the Master i.e. no leases to last for a number of peoples' lives rather than a stated period of years. The act also stated 'that the hospital shall be thereby established and confirmed for ever', its property held by it 'for ever, to be employed and bestowed to those goodly and charitable uses, for the relief and sustentation of the poor, according to the lawful orders and consideration of the foundation of the same'. The stress lies on the permanence of the institution and the inability to alienate any of its property in any way. Much of the expense of this legal activity fell on Dr. Watson's shoulders, and it was to permit him to recoup some of the costs that Queen Elizabeth allowed him to hold the bishopric and mastership at one and the same time.

Watson's work was invaluable to the Hospital. Had he not been able to regain the lost possessions, it would have been a question of strangers literally within the gates. Once he became Bishop of Winchester, he naturally was able to give less time to the running of the Hospital, but the institution does not appear to have suffered noticeably from his dual rôle.

When he died in 1583, he was succeeded at St Cross by Robert Bennett. Prior to coming to St Cross, Bennett had held the post of Chaplain to the Burlington family. In 1595 he became Dean of Windsor, a post whose royal connections made frequent attendance essential. Consequently, St Cross suffered, though his career certainly did not. He attracted sufficient attention to be appointed Bishop of Hereford in 1602, when he resigned his Mastership.

Queen Elizabeth now promised George Brooke, brother of Lord Cobham, that he should receive St Cross. Before she could complete the necessary formalities, she died. On his accession, James I set out to reward his favourites. His agent in London had been James Hudson, so he was promised the post of Master at St Cross. There was some slight doubt as to whether a layman could hold the office, as it included the benefice of St Faith. Sir Thomas Lake, who was one of James I's Secretaries of State, persuaded the King that Hudson's appointment was impossible. To make assurance doubly sure, he then bribed Hudson into resigning any right that he might have to the Hospital. Brooke revived his claim, but Sir Thomas had his own candidate—Arthur Lake, his brother, whom James appointed.

Brooke was furious at thus being passed over a second time. In consequence, he joined the Bye Plot to kidnap James and, in some fashion, take over the government. The plot was a failure. Brooke was tried for treason, found guilty and sentenced to death. A final touch of cruelty was when, at his execution, he had to mount the scaffold looking out towards St Cross, which was probably the last thing he saw in life.

Arthur Lake was a man of considerable achievements. He was a Wykehamist, with the traditional education of Winchester and New College. As a teacher, he was a fellow of Winchester, and then became Warden of New. Whilst still at St Cross he became Dean of Worcester in 1608, afterwards receiving the preferment of Bishop of Bath and Wells in 1616, when he resigned his Mastership. On occasions, he signed his surname 'du Lake', with a romantic and mythical claim to descent from one of Arthur's knights, Lancelot of the Lake.

Lake's appointment may have occurred in unfortunate circumstances, but he certainly tried to do the job in a conscientious manner. Records show that he looked after the brethren to the best of his ability, tried to use the finances for the Charity alone, and generally was an effective Master. He actually made a number of small improvements to the diet and allowances given to the brethren. Even when his work as Dean of Worcester kept him away from Winchester, he still tried to keep in touch with his charges at the Hospital.

In one other sector, Lake was conscientious. Unlike many of his predecessors, he was a frequent and earnest preacher. He is noted as having on one occasion preached 'On one doing penance for having two wives'. Quite what the relevance of this practical lesson was to the old men of St Cross is not totally clear.

King James believed in the Divine Right of Kings, and so was certain that all positions in his country could be disposed of as he saw fit. He still regarded St Cross as a plum that his favourites ought to be allowed to enjoy. When Lake moved on to Bath and Wells, he appointed his former tutor, Sir Peter Young, to the Hospital. Young had been brought up in Calvinist Geneva, but as tutor to the young prince in Scotland had built up a considerable library for James. He was a Scot, a member of James' Privy Council in his country, and had no desire to be in England. Moreover, he was a layman, though no one raised the query which had been raised in Hudson's time. Instead, he sent orders to his son, John, whom James appointed Dean of Winchester at the same time, to keep an eye on St Cross for him. Alexander Cook, writing in 1626, said of Dean Young, 'Here is £1500 offered (as it's said) for the Bishopric of Winchester, by the Dean of Winchester'. Apparently £1,500 was not enough, for he did not become Bishop, but it does give an insight into the sort of man he was.

Sir Peter rarely stirred from Fife, although there were a few occasions when he ventured to London and the court. He never, however, darkened the doors of St Cross. The Dean was equally negligent, and appointed a Mr. Wright to work as both Chaplain and Steward and do all the work. Consequently, little or nothing was done to repair the houses or look after those entitled to the charity. Fifty years later, a chaplain of the Hospital, John Hunt, wrote: 'When Sir Peter Young, a Scotchman, was Master of this Hospital, which was in the days of King James, he, living in Scotland, left the management of the concerns of this House to his sonne, Dr. Young, Dean of Winton, who made one Mr. Wright both Chaplain and Steward. This Mr. Wright dying, his widdow, whether out of fear of being brought to accounts, or out of obedience to his commands is uncertain, burnt all his papers, and amongst them, the Register also. Since which time to this there hath been no other bought. Nor could this be had, though of so small a value, without a deal of struggling and intreaty: so careless are the generality of men for public concerns, though nearly respecting them and theirs.'

The register referred to is that of births, marriages and deaths. John Hunt seems to be suggesting that he found it very difficult to persuade the parishioners of St Faith to part with a few pennies to enable him to commence a new register. Whilst not many documents of the period have survived, there are some accounts from Wright's time, from which very little can be deduced. It would seem that practically nothing was spent on the buildings for the 12 years of Young's Mastership. Perhaps Mrs. Wright felt that it would be assumed that as nothing had been spent, she and her husband had been making money out of the Hospital. Her poor financial situation would certainly deny that possibility, but it may have been sufficient motive to impel her to burn what records she could find.

After Young came Dr. Lewis, who at least had the virtue of being a 'character'. This was a royal appointment, as Winchester was temporarily without a bishop, even though Dean Young had the previous year offered a bribe for it. King Charles I presented Lewis to the Mastership in 1627 'then vacant by the natural death of Peter Young, knight'. A Welshman from Barmouth, he attended Oriel College, Oxford, where he was recognised as a scholar and organiser. As a result, he was elected Provost of his college in 1617. However, he was a ladies' man, and his activities became notorious enough for him to feel he had to give up Oxford and go abroad in 1621. Near contemporary accounts put it delightfully: 'He was implicated in some amours which became a matter of notoriety, and created great scandal and offence. He felt it necessary to withdraw himself abruptly from his provostship and retire for a time to a foreign land'. Strangely for a man with such a reputation, he was described by an Oxonian as 'very cross and disagreeable'. This might be put down to sour grapes over either his romantic or scholastic success, were it not that a later Winchester description says he was of 'a hot humour, but most loyal to His Majesty'.

Whilst overseas, he managed to retain the support of the King, and was actually used in a mission to France. This must have been a success, as he was able to return to England, safe under the monarch's wing from any worries about marauding fathers with shot guns. The King went even further, insisting that Lewis be awarded his D.D. by royal acclamation rather than from any academic effort. He became Chaplain to Charles I's favourite, Buckingham, went with him on the disastrous expedition to La Rochelle, and wrote a book about his experiences. With the support of the duke and the backing of the King, Lewis was made Master of St Cross. He went on the La Rochelle expedition less than nine months after taking up office at the Hospital, so, like many another Master before him, he began his career in *absentia*. Writing his book, too, must have taken up a fair degree of his attention and time.

Notwithstanding his reputation for hot-headedness, Lewis was happy to try to use his influence in royal circles on behalf of his friends. On 10 September 1630, he wrote to Secretary Dorchester:

> The warden of Winchester is now dead. He took his sickness in overheating himself. Pray for His Majesty's letters to the College on behalf of Mr. Robinson whom the Secretary heard preach at Beaulieu. He was schoolmaster at St Croix 14 years. Notwithstanding the great name of St Croix, the entire income is not £300 per annum. There are fallen into the Bishop of Winchester's gift, a prebend and two livings that lie conveniently for the writer. Beg the king to write to the Bishop to bestow one of the livings on him.

The last sentences show that self-interest was not entirely absent either! He was rewarded with a prebendal stall in Winchester Cathedral. The use of St Croix rather than St Cross suggests that Lewis was still thinking of France as he wrote.

This was the period of Archbishop Laud and his attempts to impose a complete unity on the Church of England. He made visits to as many dioceses as he could, and sent out detailed inquiries to the churches before his arrival. Winchester's turn for what was called 'his Grace's Metropolitical Visitation in the Diocese of Winton' came in 1632. The Articles of Enquiry at St Cross, together with the answers given, still exist today.

There were actually 16 searching questions to be answered. Occasional use of 'we' in the replies was not because Lewis claimed the prerogative of the royal 'we'. Some of the comments are made jointly by the Steward and Master, some by the Steward and Chaplain—hence the genuine use of the first person plural. The first answer established that the Bishop of Winchester had power as visitor and could take action to punish offenders against the statutes. In reply to a question about revenues and sales Lewis wrote:

The yearly rents of the House amount to £200 per annum or thereabouts; and upon our leases are reserved besides for our provision, 100 quarters of wheat, and 120 quarters of malt, and a small tithe of the parish adjoining towards the keeping of our cattle. As for wood-sales, and other extraordinary receipts, since this Master came to the place, which is now about 8 years, there have been none at all. So far from that, the Master to his great yearly charge hath been and is forced to buy at dear rates for the fuel for brewhouse, bakehouse, kitchen, hall, and his own expense; as also timber, which hath been used in great proportion, near 300 tons, for the repairs of the House: the only two woods that belong to the House having been by one of his predecessors leased out into 3 lives, and continued by the rest, which are still in being, for 6s. 8d. yearly rent; and almost all the timber trees, which were reserved, having been cut down by others, and used for fire, as some well remember.

Lewis was trying to make it plain to the visitors that, far from being an office of considerable profit, the Mastership was costing him a great deal of money. There was an immense outlay for repairs. Moreover, because people had been allowed to cut down wood which had been intended to grow into fine trees providing good wood for repair, he was having to pay over the odds for his materials. This selling off of the woods must have been a profitable business as Legh, a century before, had found it necessary to forbid the Master to sell any unnecessarily. Lewis mentions the bad habit of leasing out woods for lives, and later quotes the same bad habit with reference to other property. Consequently, there was no receipt of 'fines' which were paid on taking up a lease. This was to be a bad arrangement which plagued the Hospital until final disbandment in the 20th century. In answer to another question, Lewis goes on to point out that expenses exceed income greatly, and the loss has to be made up from his own pocket. Mention of the brewhouse and the fact that 120 quarters of malt were bought (more than the amount of wheat) suggests that the brethren were still well plied with ale as per the founder's instructions.

Asked about the number of beds, the Master quotes '13 beds for the poor, for every one a bed, of those that are to be lodged within the House'. Later, he writes 'Our Hospital doth consist of a Master and 13 Brethren, a Chaplain and Steward; 12 out-brethren, and 28 out-Sisters that are not lodged within the Hospital; and 2 Probationers'. This must be accepted as definite evidence that there were only 13 brothers living in. As they were all lumped together in one total, with no mention of differing types, it must be accepted that the brothers were all of the Hospital foundation. Forty out-liers seem to have taken the place of the Hundred Poor. The two probationers were two old men waiting patiently for someone to die so that one might step into his place.

Clearly the demand for records in earlier times was in the Master's mind when he explained that he was causing a perfect list of all the lands belonging to the Hospital to be drawn up. So far as he could see there was at that time no such list. He had also tidied up the Muniment Room and the documents in it which had 'formerly been kept in some confusion, but are nowe disposed in better order'. That documents were put into better order makes it quite certain that Mrs. Wright can only have destroyed those which referred to her husband in some fashion, as there remained the archives of other ages. It does perhaps strengthen the view that she thought that there might be the possibility of comment made over some of his dealings.

Proudly, Lewis states that the poor have had their full allowance of meat, drink, lodging and clothes 'and much more from the Master's charity, upon divers occasions and accidents, or indisposition of any of them; and attendants and physicians allowed them in their sickness, and diet at the Master's charge, which is not provided for by the Statute. We know not of any thing wherein the Master hath offended. And if, at any time, any of the Officers or Alsmfolk have offended, they have been punished by the Master.'

Although church services were regularly held on Sundays, Holy Days, and week days, a sermon was not always given. Lewis reports, 'Sermons we have at all the chief Festivals of the year, preached by the Master, and often at other times as his occasions permit'. This does not square with the picture that many now have of long sermons in Laudian times and the Protectorate, but rather of a man boasting that he actually preached at all.

The catalogue of repairs shows clearly how much the Hospital had been allowed to fall into modified ruin by the neglect of men like Young.

> The fabrick of our Church and House, both which are very large, and all outhouses (which were all found by this Master in great ruin and delapidation, towards which he received no allowance from his predecessor) are now in better repair than they have been within the memory of man. The chancel and the two adjoining aisles of the church new rooft and leaded, and two aisles more adjoining to the body of the church and chancel likewise new rooft and covered: the windows of the church and chancel, which were for the most part stopt with board and mortar, new barred and glazed; and organ set up therein; the church, as also the cellar and other offices, newly paved; the four sides of the quadrangle stript and newly tiled; the brewhouse and bakehouse wholly stript and tiled, and newly repaired both with walls and timber; the barns and stables, and all the walls about the House beautified within and without, to the Master's great charge: wherein he hath expended out of his own purse, as appeareth by the Steward's accounts, about one thousand pounds, having had no extraordinary receipt by casualty, fine, or otherwise, towards his so extraordinary a charge; and yet much left to do about the Church and House.

Dr. Lewis' claim to have spent the money from his private purse is borne out by the accounts. He must have been a wealthy man to be able to have spent so much of his own capital. His comment that he had made the place better than living man could remember is certainly true. Lake, who definitely looked after the brethren in a conscientious manner, was not nearly so careful over the state of repair of the buildings. Young, of course, had ignored both. Again, it is hard to convert Stuart money into modern terms, but something over a quarter of a million pounds expended is not unfair. Here is yet another example in the history of St Cross of robber Masters leaving the place in desperate need of repair, and a well-intentioned man spending his own wealth to bring it back on to an even keel. Probably, the better administration and greater care of property would have meant that, in time, the Hospital would be able to meet its commitments. This would then have meant that Dr. Lewis would have been able to expect some recompense for his considerable expenditure.

Of interest is the introduction of an organ. This ties up with the Chanter and singing man who put their names on a stall in 1572. The early reformers had tried to drive out chanting as a popish device, but by now Cathedrals were beginning to reintroduce choirs.

Even so, St Cross could reasonably claim to be one step ahead with its organ. Clearly the Hospital was determined to retain its tradition of being musical. Another sign of the Hospital's determined independence is the fact that from at least 1580 it allowed Catholics to bury their dead in the churchyard of St James. This was hallowed ground and so, in the church politics of the time, only Protestants should use it. Watson's more liberal approach was followed by other Masters for another two centuries.

One thing the Laud's visitation insisted upon. All over the country, the Archbishop's agents were pointing out that there were too many altars or communion tables. They sought to impose a uniformity of practice on the Church of England. In future there must only be the one altar in the chancel at the east end of the church, and that must be protected by rails 'one yard in height and so thick with pillars that dogs may not get in'. What a picture of church usage this gives—the need to lay down an overall rule that dogs must be kept away from the altar! There was no need to oppose this reduction to one altar, in Dr. Lewis' mind, and so St Cross lost its multiplicity of altars around the church. Clear signs of piscinas for the officiating priest to wash his hands, next to where some of the altars had stood, can still be found in transepts and chapels.

CHAPTER *IX*
Revolution and Restoration

T he Stuart age was one in which the rich Protestant gentry spent a great deal of their money on the foundation of residential charities for the poor of their neighbourhood, or took part in schemes to provide employment for those without work. Professor Jordan estimates that, while there were perhaps fifty-five residential charities at the end of Elizabeth's reign, by the end of James II's rule the number had risen to about two hundred and twenty. Professor Tawney comments on the growing support for existing church-based charities, as well as the growth of new ones. What is interesting is that St Cross did not benefit from this particular flow of funds. Presumably it was still regarded as a 'plum' post and able to provide for itself from its current endowments. Certainly, the Stuarts and the Commonwealth appointed their favourites to be Master, as with Dr. Lewis himself and his successor, Lisle.

Dr. Lewis was unfortunate that he lived in the days of the Civil War and that his allegiance was to the losing side. Although the reasons which prompted him to leave England for the first time, and the unfortunate temper which he possessed, do him no great credit, his firm and unswerving loyalty to the King was wholly admirable. Everyone in Winchester knew him as a strong royalist. When the monarchy ended and the republic was declared, Lewis could no longer remain in the country. He was almost certainly in some danger from the puritans, but his own conscience would not let him live in a country that executed its King. Accordingly, he once more went to France, there to join many more royalists in difficult circumstances.

One of the actions of the Commonwealth parliament was to abolish the office of bishop—therefore there was apparently no one who could make an appointment to replace the Master of St Cross. John Lisle was at that time M.P. for Winchester, a position which he had held throughout the Long Parliament. Although the city's loyalties wavered at times from parliamentarian to royalist, Lisle remained a stern republican at all times. He was one of the two commissioners who sat alongside Bradshaw, the president of the court, at the trial of Charles I, in order to give legal advice. When there was some doubt as to whether the King had first to be deposed and then tried and sentenced, Lisle was one of seven commissioners who ensured that the trial and sentencing went ahead without waste of time. Finally, he signed Charles' death warrant. At the Restoration he was especially exempted from parliament's act of indemnity, and all his property was confiscated, whilst Winchester expelled him from its corporation. He fled to Lausanne in Switzerland; but vengeance followed him, and he was stabbed to death by an Irish royalist whilst on his way to church. A more gory account has him being shot by one man and then ridden over by two others on horseback. Despite his place in history, he is probably better known in Winchester as the husband of Alice, who was so bullied at her trial by Judge Jeffrey and was executed for harbouring some of Monmouth's men at the time of the rising against James II.

Lisle felt happy in the legal argument that, as the law-making body had abolished bishops, it was perfectly reasonable for someone from that body to take the place of the prelate in Winchester and make the appointment to St Cross. So he appointed himself and took over at once. He also saw no reason why he should not change the conditions for entry, as, after all, these had been laid down by bishops, who no longer had legal existence. Therefore he decided that the Hospital should be used to pension off parliamentary soldiers. No longer was there a rule about being weak and unable to look after oneself. Some of the soldiers admitted must have been younger than the usual entrant to St Cross. For instance, in 1373 a Winchester College record notes men aged 60, 65 and 70 and two of over 80 in the institution. Soldiers were enlisted for life, but in the Civil War many were merely 'in for the duration' and were presumably quite young men when they returned to civilian status. Unfortunately the ages of those entered into the Hospital is not known, although a certain James Marshall is noted as being 'on [sic] of Cromwell's men'. This may even mean that he was one of the Ironsides, but it certainly shows that Lisle's plan did bear some fruit. This connection with the victorious army may be one of the main reasons why St Cross survived the Protectorate when so many other Winchester institutions were closed. Only the College, St John's Hospital, and Symonds Hospital, apart from St Cross, appear to have escaped the axe.

Lisle was a stern Puritan, and anything that nearly approached Roman Catholicism had to go. It must be remembered that, although 'puritan' had been used as a term of abuse for some time, the everyday appellation of 'precisians' was used at least as often, since the group was so precise (perhaps over-precise) in its conduct and doctrine. Some of the stained-glass windows at St Cross were taken out and replaced with plain glass. The original stained glass was often preserved and put away safely, but one result of the removals is the splendidly mixed glass replaced in the south-east window of the north transept at the time of the Restoration. As a matter of fact, scarcely one piece of medieval glass is now in its original position in any part of the church.

Another removal was the statue of the Virgin Mary on the eastern pillar of the northern aisle. This was doubly disliked as it was claimed to have been specially placed where the first rays of the sun fell on it at dawn on Holy Cross day, and so seemed to Lisle to smack of both idolatry and sun worship. There are also certain niches which used to contain, using the biblical phrase, 'graven images', presumably of saints, which are now empty. Pillars bear the marks of the removal of other images.

A story is told that Lisle also ordered the removal of the statue of the Virgin Mary in the Beaufort Tower. The brethren explained that it was not the Virgin Mary. Any fool could see that it was a young maiden carrying a milk pail on her head and a babe in her arms. She clearly represented the legendary girl who had persuaded de Blois to found the order. Lisle is said to have been convinced; at any rate he left the statue alone. Possibly its salvation lay in the fact that it was more difficult to remove than any other of the 'idols'.

Another target for destruction was the lectern. With such a mixed parentage, it could only be looked upon as some sort of magical bird. Puritans could not accept witchcraft and magic, so the bird had to go. The local worker bidden to the task pointed out that the wooden piece was really too heavy to cart out in one, and obtained permission to cut it into two pieces. He then took it away and buried it in St Faith's churchyard, where the

29 *The lectern. Note the cut in the legs and the variation in colour of the wood at the joint.*

digging of holes was only to be expected. At the Restoration, the lectern was dug up, put together, and returned to its place of honour in the church. Certainly, the cut can be seen plainly to this day and the woodwork has two different colours, perhaps from having been buried at different depths or in different kinds of soil.

A yet further sufferer was the organ. Singing and music had been maintained at the Hospital in the difficult days of the early reformation. Cromwell's parliament passed a law ordering the removal of organs as 'squeaking abominations'. So St Cross lost its organ after less than one hundred years of work.

Lisle was a sincere man. He made very little out of his post as Master. The evidence of the accounts would suggest a maximum payment of £200 per annum. On the other hand, he did increase the amounts of relief given to the non-resident almsfolk, and appears to have looked after the residents with a paternal, if strict, eye. There is clear evidence, too, that the church continued to be used by the locals as a parish church, at least in some respects. There are two sad little memorial stones to the Laurence children, one just two years old, and the other barely one. The long-standing English difficulty with spelling names continued as the first to die is spelt 'Laurence' whilst the second has been raised to the Latin in 'Laurentius'. Both use the Latin *vixit* for born and the less usual *devixit* for died, instead of *obiit*—stressing life from beginning to end. 'Susana' has a three word Latin epitaph, translated underneath it in ten words of English. 'Georgius' gets four words of Latin, which English raises to six. They are surely good advertisements for the concise quality of Latin prose.

Generally, the Commonwealth officers felt that there were too many churches and possible priests in the area. A report of 1650 suggested that St Cross parish (strictly, a non-existent entity) should be joined with St Lawrence. In the event, nothing was done.

Oliver Cromwell found ruling England through the Commons was a particularly difficult task. After declining the offer of the crown, he added an 'Other House' of members nominated by him to parliament. One of the men chosen for this House (really the House of Lords under another name) was John Lisle. He did not think that he could carry out his duties at St Cross and support Cromwell in London at the same time, and so resigned office in 1657.

The importance assigned by the Protectorate to the Hospital may be gauged from the man who was sent to follow Lisle. He was John Cooke, another of the regicides. Part visionary, part practical reformer, he had drawn up the charge against Charles I and acted as Prosecutor. One of his ideas for improving matters nationally was that no alcohol should be allowed, but that the poor should have free medical and legal services. There would no doubt be some opposition to the first suggestion amongst the brethren at St Cross! It is, however, a far-sighted suggestion of a precursor of the Welfare State. As the Protectorate was drawing to its close, he was appointed Chief Justice Minister in Ireland in 1659—some of the modern-day troubles derive from his actions in support of Protestants there. He at once resigned as Master of St Cross.

Richard Cromwell, who, with his Hursley connections, was virtually local to St Cross, succeeded his father as Protector. He appointed Richard Shute to take over the Hospital when Cooke went to Ireland. Shortly afterwards, Cromwell decided that ruling was not his *métier* and quit office. Cooke was taken prisoner by royalists, later to be tried and executed, and Charles II prepared to come back into his own.

Once the monarchy was restored, the Commonwealth Master could not hope to hold his place, so Shute quietly resigned and left Winchester. It is worth noting that none of the three men who held office under the Republic was a complete absentee, and that when other duties meant long periods of absence, they at once vacated their post.

Amongst the many royalists now returning to England in triumph after the hard times of their exile was Dr. Lewis. As far as he was concerned, there was no problem in St Cross. There had been no bishops under the Commonwealth, so no one could have been collated to the office he held. He had merely been forced to be absent from his duties, to which he now returned as of right. To him, there had never been a time when he was not Master of St Cross. Naturally, the restored monarchy agreed with him, and he moved back into the Master's lodge. This has led to some lists of Masters omitting

30 *John Cooke, Master of St Cross 1657-1659.*

entirely the three men who officiated under the Commonwealth, because they had never been properly appointed. As they did more actual work than many of those before and after them who were so installed, it is clearly ridiculous to leave them out.

Lewis remained Master for a further seven years. In his time, led by Peter Gorham, the Roman Catholics began once more to practise their faith publicly in Winchester. By 1676, according to a survey drawn up by order of Henry Compton, then Bishop of London, but formerly Master of St Cross, there were 243 practising Catholics in Winchester, as against 4,545 'conformists' and 177 of all types of nonconformists. As a staunch royalist, Dr. Lewis had seen the support given to the King by Catholics and was prepared to accept them. He was well aware of the tradition amongst Masters (though not under the Protectorate) of turning a blind eye to the burials of Catholics in St James, land which had first come to the Hospital in the days of Beaufort. He now returned to that practice, which had been disrupted by Cromwell's rule, and is said even to have gone further and almost encouraged Catholics to look on St James as their place of burial by right. Apart from feeling that the Catholics had earned his support because of their attitude to the King, his broad church approach may well have been affected by his family, for his wife, Alice, is said to have been a Roman Catholic and was herself buried in St James' burial ground in 1677. A mild coincidence is the fact that both he and Lisle had wives called Alice, both were survived by their wives, and both found their wives on differing sides of either the religious or political fence. In *Fasti Oxoniensis* it is recorded that the Master's sons also became converts to Catholicism. Peter Bogan records that one of them, Theodore, became a Jesuit and Chaplain at Brambridge.

Another point, which seems to suggest a form of ecumenical approach by Lewis, is the fact that none of the republican ex-soldiers was turned out of the Hospital. With his long record of total support for the King, one would expect the good doctor to turn out the evil republicans to make room for deserving cases amongst impoverished royalists, of whom there were many. It is to his credit that he took no such action, nor does he appear even to have considered it. There is evidence of a real desire to look after the men under his care. In 1663, he appointed Dr. Taylor, a leading physician in Winchester, to be doctor to them. Taylor did not take his duties seriously, and very rarely visited the Hospital, although he drove around the city in his coach and four, and was thus totally mobile. When he died, he left an estate worth the enormous amount of £18,000.

Lewis himself died in July 1667 and is buried inside the church, just before the high altar. His elegant Latin epitaph suggests that his troubles had mellowed him. He is remembered as having taught Christianity effectively and to have lived according to its precepts. He maintained an unswerving loyalty to his King, and had been neither elated by prosperity nor put down by adversity. All in all, a splendid man of a mild temper, who became not only Master of St Cross but also a canon of Winchester Cathedral. Certainly, no one at any time would query his loyalty to his King, but the points about preaching and mild temper might possibly have raised some eyebrows amongst his contemporaries at Oxford, Winchester, or in the King's service.

Chapter X

The Consuetudinarium

Under Lewis, the Hospital may be said to have quietly jogged along. No great innovations and no dreadful despoliations occurred. Almost certainly, the Master spent his time within and around St Cross, basically attending to his duties. Henry Compton, his successor, was, like Lewis, rewarded for family services to the King, but he was a man of very different character. One of the sons of the Earl of Northampton, who had been killed in the Civil War, Compton was given the post of Master at St Cross in recognition of his father's loyalty. His first love had been the army, and he became a Cornet of Horse in the Horse Guards. However, he did not make the progress he hoped for, and so turned to that refuge of younger sons of the nobility, the Church. He never lost his love of things military, and, at the time of the overthrow of King James II, when he was already a bishop, led a body of horsemen who carried Princess Anne off to safety.

Compton's first living was that of Cottenham in Cambridgeshire. St Cross became vacant in 1667, and the circumstances of his father's death, coupled with his position as tutor to the Princesses Mary and Anne (both future Queens of England), ensured that he obtained promotion to it. In fact, Compton came to the post as the nominee of the Archbishop of Canterbury, who had reserved it as his option. Whilst still at St Cross, in the usual style of plural livings, he also held the canonry of Christchurch and the see of Oxford, plus, of course, his royal appointments. He must have found it very difficult to fit in time for the Hospital in his crowded schedule, although he was not an entirely absent Master.

When he was appointed Bishop of London in 1675, he resigned St Cross and plunged into the troubled religious and political life of the times. His family connections meant that almost inevitably he would have been drawn in, but his strong Protestantism brought him constantly into conflict with the growing catholicism of James II's views. When William and Mary seized the throne, he carried out the act of coronation, as the Archbishop of Canterbury, Sancroft, refused to do so.

Royal interest in the disposal of St Cross continued to be strong after Compton's resignation. Bishop Morley, as Visitor, nominated William Harrison to be Master of the Hospital in February 1675. It was pointed out that the King had the right of presentation at this stage, and Harrison's appointment was declared invalid, only to be confirmed by the King in May. Once the proper order had been maintained, all was well. Meanwhile, Harrison acted as Master from the end of February, regardless of the slight irregularity. His brother apparently held the living of Crondal, which was part of St Cross's patrimony, with at least the collusion of the Master.

Whilst Harrison was in office, Wren produced his great plan for a new royal palace in Winchester. One section envisaged a park of 10 miles in circumference, stretching out from the old castle area. All owners of land in that area were forbidden either to re-lease or renew leases for any land that fell within the possible park. This, of course, affected St Cross. Perhaps Harrison's attitude may be gauged from the fact that he was noted as being at the horse racing in Winchester in 1683, an event also attended by Charles II. Even though he was the King's nominee, it is highly improbable that he was actually one of his majesty's party. Much more likely is the fact that he heard that Charles was going racing and decided to go himself, in the hope that he might just be noticed. This was also the year in which the foundation stone of this huge palace-to-be was laid, though little else was completed. At any rate, there is no record of Harrison having raised even a squeak in opposition.

The military side of the Hospital was maintained in this period. One of the brothers installed was John Starkey. He was a Cheshire man who had served abroad for 30 years, and had then been for 10 years in 'His Majesty's Guards'. At about this time, Charles embodied a regiment of Foot Guards from soldiers who had served in Spain. It is possible, therefore, that Starkey was one of the original Foot Guards in England. They had a real duty of protecting the King's life, as well as fighting in the forefront in his wars. This royal soldier must have acted as a balance against the Cromwellian troops brought in.

There was still a variety in those who entered St Cross under Harrison. Sir Edward Richards, knight, died as a brother of the Hospital in January 1685. Another man who might have qualified, like Richards, as one of Beaufort's brothers had they still existed, was William Coles. He worked as clerk and Porter for the Hospital in his time as brother. He had been an alderman and Mayor of Romsey 'but, meeting with misfortune, he met with a peaceful asylum within the walls of the Hospital'.

The accounts of this period make it fairly certain that the old habit of feeding the hundred poor had died. It would appear that, perhaps as early as the days of Lisle, the system had changed. There was probably some feeding of the poor, but certainly not to a total of one hundred. None of the accounts would suggest purchase of sufficient food to provide meals for them. Also, there were now disbursements of money to poor people who lived outside the grounds, in a complete reversal of the orders laid down at the visitation of Dr. Legh. Harrison certainly catered for what he called 'out-pensioners'.

Another fact, which becomes clear from examining the expenditure of the times, is that Harrison was not greatly worried about the state of repair of the buildings. His sons seem to have had equally little concern. On two of the pillars to the windows in the Hall are to be found, carved into the stone, the names of the young men, one of whom particularly mentions that he is 'George, the eldest son of Dr. Harrison'. Graffiti is not new! Whilst the Master spent money on feeding and looking after his charges, there was no big repair work undertaken. This is a failing that can be noted in a number of Masters, who could reasonably have claimed to have done their work conscientiously, and not to have robbed the Charity's funds.

In 1694, on Harrison's death, Abraham Markland succeeded to the post of Master of St Cross. Although he obtained a D.D., he was said to be more interested in literature than divinity. When he came to Hampshire, it was with the avowed intention of 'pursuing the pleasing paths of poetry and mathematics'. Apart from St Cross, he was also rector of

Meonstoke and prebendary of Winchester Cathedral. His wife, daughter of Mr. Pitt of Stratfield Saye, was a member of the aristocratic Rivers family. He thus had strong connections outside the Hospital.

Markland found himself involved with queries over the late Dr. Harrison's estate. His widow, Mrs. Harrison, was also his executrix. She claimed the tithes and other payments that were due at the time of her husband's death, 'and the hay cut and divided from the Glebe and the barley that was sowed by the said Dr. Harrison'. It was easily accepted that the tithes etc. due at the time of death should go to his estate. There was an argument as to whether grass growing, but not cut, and barley sowed, but not ripened, should be treated in the same manner. In the end, the courts found for Mrs. Harrison.

Soon after his arrival, Markland found the quarters assigned to the Master in the tower to be uncomfortable and difficult of access. Each of the rooms had windows to north and south, and a huge fireplace supposedly warmed them. Those who have worked in the rooms would readily agree that they did not produce the highest levels of comfort. However, they were, and are, extensive and imposing. In 1696, Markland had a number of the brethren's rooms along the north side of the quad pulled down, and re-fashioned to form a rather more comfortable Master's lodging. This building, be it noted, was completed at a time when little or no other maintenance work was being done. As a result, there were now no brethren's rooms on either the east or north sides of the inner quadrangle, all being concentrated on the west and a short sector of the south.

Soon after taking up office, Markland found himself in dispute with the Chaplain, Steward, brethren—indeed, everyone within the Hospital—over what were their duties and privileges. He decided to produce a written statement which would clarify all the necessary points. Before embarking on this work, he claimed to have searched high and low for original statutes to help him, but was not successful. There must be some doubt over this claim, as the documents still exist within St Cross archives and were extensively quoted from in the Chancery action of the 19th century. As there were no statutes, Markland claimed that the Hospital had always been run by custom and by examining the terms of any grants and donations. He thus turned to the brethren who had been longest in St Cross, and to Mr. Complin, then 72 years old, who had been Steward for over thirty years. With their help, he drew up the Consuetudinarium, better known as 'The Custumary'. This is so important in the next 100 years, as the document by which the Hospital was ruled, that it is worth quoting extensively from it.

The Custumary explains that

> the said Hospital doth consist of one Master, 13 brethren, one Steward and one Chaplain, and as an additional Charity there is the Hundred Hall consisting of eight and twenty poor women and twelve poor men, and there are two others called reversioners who usually succeed upon the death or vacancy of any of the former. That it hath been the custom and usage and now is that the Master should rule and govern all persons in and belonging to the said Hospital, and receive either by himself or his Steward all the profits and revenues thereof, with which he is to bear the whole charge of the house in manner hereafter particularly expressed, and to keep the Church and the House in sufficient repair, and the surplus, if any there be, he is to retain to himself, and he is to keep the common seal of the said Hospital, and with it in the Common

Hall, with the consent of the major part of the brethren, to seal all Leases and Grants of any Lands or tenements belonging to the Hospital, and he is to have to his own use all the goods and personal estate of every Brother dying whether such goods or personal Estate were in the possession of such brother so dying, or were in the possession of any other person.

This was an extremely important clause. It meant that all the money coming to the Charity was at the disposal of the Master. So long as he could persuade himself that he was looking after the brethren and just about keeping the buildings upright, he could pocket any surplus for his own use. He was entitled to all the goods and chattels of any brother dying within the Hospital walls. There was some justification for claiming this as a custom, since Pare shows in his accounts the receipt of 22s. 6d for the 'goods of divers brothers deceased'. Obviously, rogues such as de Cloune would have been delighted to have had their actions thus made legal.

Next came a clause giving total right of appointment of both Steward and Chaplain, as well as all brethren, to the Master alone. He was also given the right to turn out of the Hospital or from the number of the Hundred Menne's Hall anyone he thought to be guilty of 'misdemeanours, and heinous and grave offences'. He was, indeed, monarch of all he surveyed. Food was clearly important and some long passages deal with it.

For their bread and beer, each shall have a pint of beer and a piece of bread at Eight of o'clock in the morning, a Quart of beer and a piece of bread at Dinner, a pint of beer and a piece of bread at three of the clock in the afternoon, and a quart of beer and a piece of bread at supper. But for their conveniences [sic] and at their request, they all take their bread and beer in the morning, to wit, each of them takes three quarts of beer a day for himself and five casts and a half of bread are divided daily among them. They have also forty-six and half pounds of beef and forty-six and a half pounds of mutton allowed them by the week, part whereof is boiled to make broath, and other part thereof, that is upon Sunday nights, is roaste.

The immediate response to this diet is that presumably no teetotaller was ever invited to become a brother.

Markland's original document laid down in detail what was to be received on special days.

That there are five festival days in the year, to wit—All Saints, Christmas, New Year's Day, Twelfth Day, and Candlemas Day: on which the brethren have extraordinary commons, and on the eve of which days they have a fire of charcoal in the Common Hall, and one jack of six quarts and one pint of beer extraordinary to drink together by the fire. And on the said Feast Days they have a fire at dinner, and another at supper in the said hall; and they have a sirloin of beef roasted, weighing forty-six pounds and a half, and three large mince pies, and plum broth, and three joints of mutton for their supper, and six quarts and one pint of beer extraordinary at dinner, and six quarts and one pint of beer after dinner, by the fireside; six quarts and one pint at supper, and the like after supper. And on Wednesdays before Shrove Tuesdays at dinner every brother hath a pancake; and on Shrove Tuesdays at dinner every brother hath a pancake besides his commons of beef, and six quarts and one pint of beer extraordinary, among them all; and at supper their mutton is roasted, and three hens roasted, and six quarts and one pint of beer extraordinary. And in Lent time every brother hath in lieu of his commons eight shillings in money paid. And on Palm Sunday the brethren have a green fish, of the value of three shillings and four pence, and their pot of milk pottage with three pounds of rice boiled in it, and three pies with twenty-four herrings baked in them, and six quarts and one pint of beer extraordinary. And they have on Good Friday, at dinner, in their pot of beer a cast of bread sliced, and three pounds of honey, boiled together, which they call honey sop. Also every brother receives quarterly eight shillings: viz, six shillings and eightpence for himself, and sixteen pence to pay his laundress; and four shillings paid among them by the tenants of Yately. Also, there is allowed by the Master three shillings and fourpence quarterly to a barber, for the trimming of the brothers. And upon sealing and renewing of leases each brother is to have twopence in the pound, for so many pounds as the fine for renewing the lease amounts to. And at Christmas, yearly, every brother shall have a new gown made of black cloth rash, of five shillings the yard.

The mince pies were not those we are accustomed to looking for at Christmas, but pies of minced meat. They must have been of very considerable size, as the ingredients are quoted as being 'two legs of mutton (12lb. weight), 6lb. beef suet, 3 gallons of fine flour, 3lb. of butter, 3lb. of currants, 3lb. of sun raisins'. The plum broth apparently consisted of '2lb. of prunes, 1oz. of nutmeg, 1oz. of ginger, 1oz. of cloves, 1oz. of mace, 1lb. of sugar'. Spicy, to say the least!

As far as the Hundred Menne's Hall poor were concerned, Markland seems to go half-way to feeding them:

The custom there was, and had been from time out of memory, that the Hundred Hall should consist of forty poor men and women, namely, twelve poor men and twenty-eight poor women, and two reversioners, who were to receive from the Steward every Sunday 1d. each, and were to have four sheep's hinges, and soup made for them of the hinges every Sunday, Tuesday, and Thursday, to be divided among them in the room called Hundred hall; and also on those days a peck of wheat of the house-made bread, made and baked into forty little loaves; that they were to have a barrel of beer every time they brewed for the house, and that the twenty-eight women were to have on Fridays, for dinner, milk pottage and three and a half casts of wheat bread, and one pint of beer each, and in Lent a peck of peas boiled in lieu of the sheep's hinge at dinner, and 9d each in lieu of the herrings formerly allowed them in Lent. That it was the custom that there should be three bushels of malt toll free for every hogshead of beer; and that the Porter was to receive every day from the Butler a cast of bread and three quarts of beer, to relieve at the gate such poor persons as came and craved relief there. That it was the custom that there should be six doles in the year, namely, Christmas Eve, Easter Eve, the 3rd. May, finding of the Holy Cross, Whitsun Eve, the 10th. August, the founder's obit, and the Eve of All Saints, on which days there were to be distributed among such as should come for them, in little loaves, eight bushels of wheaten bread, amounting to between 700 and 800, and if the number of people should be more than the number of loaves should suffice, then the Steward was to give to every other person one half-penny in lieu thereof. All which customs and usages the said Master, Brethren, Steward and Chaplain did respectfully and jointly promise to observe and keep.

Provisions were also made for the officers of the Hospital:

> That it hath been the custom and usage, and now is, that there should be a Steward
> of the said Hospital, who is appointed by the Master for the time being. And, upon
> his entrance into the Stewardship, he is to take the oath of the House to be faithful
> and true to the Master and Brethren; and to receive the rents, pensions, and all dues
> and profits belonging to the Hospital; and from time to time to pay the Chaplain,
> Brethren, Hundred Hall, and all others belonging to the said Hospital; and upon
> demand, to give the Master a true account thereof. In the said Master's absence he
> directs and governs all things and all persons in the said Hospital; and he hath power
> to punish any of the Brethren and Hundred hall, for any misdemeanour, by sconsing
> them their commons. He ought to have a chamber in the said Hospital, with conven-
> ient furniture, fire and candle, by the Master's appointment; and he is to have his diet
> with the Master, and in his absence to diet with the Chaplain. He is to have a salary
> of eight pounds thirteen shillings and four pence per annum, to be paid him quarterly.

To those accustomed to a modern sconsing involving large amounts to drink, taken
rapidly, this use of the word is almost the opposite. It means that the rations may be cut
down. Similarly, 'diet with the Chaplain' does not mean that both men had less to eat
when the Master was away, but merely that they ate together.

As far as the Chaplain went, the Custumary stated:

> That it hath been the custom and usage, and now is, that there should be a Chaplain
> in the said Hospital, to be appointed by the Master for the time being, who is to be
> in orders of the Church of England. His duty is to read prayers in the Church twice
> a day, to visit the sick in the parish adjoining and in the Hospital, and to assist the
> Master on all necessary occasions. He is to have a chamber in the Hospital, with
> convenient furniture, fire, and candle, by the Master's appointment; and to diet with
> the Master, but in his absence with the Steward. His salary is ten pounds a year, to
> be paid quarterly.

The implication here is that all matters to do with the church had to be attended
to by the Chaplain, whilst the Master was more in the position of a lay estate owner.

On the other hand, the ecclesiastical side of the appointment was recognised by
asking the Bishop of Winchester to ratify the document. This may have been because
Markland accepted the Bishop as Visitor to the Hospital, or simply because that, as a
clergyman, he recognised himself as being under discipline to his ecclesiastical superior.
On 10 July 1696, Bishop Mews duly gave his blessing, adding 'always intending that
nothing herein shall be construed to derogate from the Statutes of the Founder, if any such
shall appear'. He also instructed that the Custumary should be read aloud in the presence
of the Master, Brethren, Steward, and Chaplain, annually on 3 May, the Invention of the
Holy Cross. Thus, the whole document received the episcopal sign of approval, and
became recognised as the quasi-legal instrument through which the Hospital should be
run. It is noticeable that nowhere in the Custumary is there any mention of the Order
of Noble Poverty.

Markland was now fully entitled to feel that he could run the Hospital on the basis
of his Custumary and to consider that it should be a place of profit to him. That this was
so, and that it involved some ignoring of necessary repair work, is shown by this extract

from Defoe's *A Journey Through England* published in 1723, in the section London to Land's End, letter 3.

> The hospital on the south of this city, at a mile's distance on the road to Southampton, is worth notice. 'Tis said to be founded by King William Rufus, but was not endowed or appointed till later times by Cardinal Beaufort. Every traveller that knocks at the door of this house, in his way, and asks for it, claims the relief of a piece of white bread and a cup of beer; and this donation is still continued; a quantity of good beer is set apart every day to be given away; and what is left is distributed to other poor, but none of it is kept to the next day.

> How the revenues of this hospital, which should maintain the master and thirty private gentlemen, who they call fellows, but ought to call brothers, is now reduced to maintain only fourteen, while the master lives in a figure equal to the best gentlemen in the country, would be well worth the enquiry of a proper visitor, if such can be named. 'Tis a thing worthy of complaint, when public charities, designed for the relief of the poor, are embezzled and deprecated by the rich, and turned to the support of luxury and pride.

Defoe has clearly not heard of the original, de Blois, Foundation, although that is what he describes, but his writings make it clear that first call on the institution's funds was the Master. Despite this, it must in fairness be pointed out that the new Custumary did increase the money paid to the brothers by about a quarter. Markland also amended the stipend for Chaplains in 1725 when Rev. Thomas Williams succeeded Rev. Keble White. Williams received £20 per annum, plus £16 for his food, a cord of wood, 100 faggots, and his candles. At this time, it was estimated that the Master received about £600 per annum.

As befitted a man who was a scholar—a member of St John's, Oxford at 17— Markland was apparently a frequent and eloquent preacher. His preaching extended to the congregations of St Faith, who were still attached to St Cross, and Meonstoke, which he held in pluralcy. Preaching at Meonstoke shows a rather more conscientious attitude than many of his confreres, for plural livings were usually ignored or left entirely to poorly paid curates. He was also an enthusiastic gardener, in the sense that he ensured that the gardens around the Hospital, as well as the Master's garden, were well maintained by the staff. They thus became a place of beauty which brethren could enjoy, although they did also grow some produce for the table. Whilst repair work was not regarded highly, internal decoration of a sort was. It is recorded in the burial register that he completed the complete white-washing of the church three weeks before he died at the age of 83. Later generations spent immense time and energy in removing the evidence of his work, although an architect's report of 1920 advised whitewashing the whole once more. Perhaps Markland was right in his work, and all that energy expended later could have been saved.

Dr. Markland's memorial stone, close by the altar rail, proudly records his work in the gardens and notes that he raised the 'stipend' of the brothers. 'As a preacher, he was diliugent [sic], eloquent and persuasive ... he was especially noted for the suavity of his manners and his universal benevolence'. His care of the brothers was most fatherly in spirit. He is praised '*summa cum laude*'. His wife's memorial stone records that she died 'not of apoplexy, but ecstasy' on her way to church.

After Markland came John Lynch, of whom not much is reported, except that he was reputed to be the greatest pluralist of the 18th century. He was 'an Archbishop's option' to St Cross, so it is possible that his connections in the right places may have meant that he was well rewarded. If this is so, it was a title as pluralist won against some considerable opposition. He certainly left a very definite physical mark on the Hospital. In 1737, he arranged for William Skelthorp, a London clock maker, to install a clock in the church tower. In the days when few people had a watch and very few had access to a clock, this must have been an asset to both the village and Hospital.

Lynch was responsible for the first change in the Custumary. Pleading that the church was a very wet place, 'and the brethren thereof very ancient men unable to attend evening prayer without manifest hazard and danger of their health and life', he obtained permission to reduce the number of daily services from two to one, in the morning at eleven o'clock. As a sop to Cerberus, he agreed that a sermon should be preached every Sunday, instead of alternate weeks, for the benefit of the villagers, because the village of St Cross had grown in numbers. He carefully made the point that the parishioners of St Faith had no other place for worship, and 'they are permitted to attend' St Cross. The word 'permitted' is important as it shows that Lynch did not regard St Cross as a parish church. As the Bishop of Winchester had to give his consent to these changes, it is clear that he, too, held the same opinion.

That the Hospital was able to attract men of ability is also shown by one of the men who was Steward at this time. From 1741-1752, under Lynch, Thomas Wylde was Steward. When he left St Cross, he moved to be Head of the High School in Nottingham. He must have been a scholar of some note to have been able to obtain such a post so far from his home at a time of poor roads and postal communication.

In 1760, by virtue of being Bishop Hoadly's son, John Hoadly became Master of St Cross. The Bishop was a great believer in spreading the ecclesiastical favours around his family, though not quite so keen on being actually in Winchester. John became Chancellor of the diocese, and held Alresford and two other rectories. He was also a playwright; David Garrick acted in his *The Suspicious Husband*. Before becoming Master, he was appointed Chairman of the Winchester Hospital, which was England's first provincial hospital. He was not a great Master, having somewhat similar views to his father with regard to attendance. He wrote to his friend, Hogarth, that he occasionally visited his parishes as the shepherd ought to be seen sometimes amongst his flock, if only to fleece them. With the Custumary to support him, Hoadly sat back and took what he could from St Cross. In 1763, he, with other churchmen, 'did take with them several experienced workmen and did then and there view and survey' all the buildings. They came to the conclusion that the buildings running from the Porter's lodge to the church (the ambulatory, infirmary, and nuns' rooms) were all in a very bad state. It would cost a great deal to repair them, and even then they would really be useless and 'a further incumbrance'. He appealed to the Bishop, by then John Thomas, for faculty to pull them down. The idea was that the materials from those buildings would then be used to repair others within the Hospital. This was granted, but fortunately Hoadly did not have the energy in any of his visits to set this in motion, and the buildings still stand as a memorial to past ages.

31 *Saint Cross in 1760, before the south wing of brethren's quarters was pulled down.*

Another 'Archbishop's option' came in 1776, when Beilby Porteus was 'admitted and instituted to the office of master and Guardian' of St Cross. The phrase 'master and Guardian' has a good ring to it and shows that Porteus was expected to defend the rights and properties of the Hospital and not despoil it. On 12 June 1782, the Bishop decided to abolish the old oath on taking office and substitute a new one. Porteus was required to take the new oath, which ran: 'I do swear that I will well and truly observe fulfil and keep all the constitutions, laudable customs, and usages of the Hospital of St Cross together with the observations made therein by the Authority of the Visitor'. This oath made the position of the Bishop as Visitor quite secure, but really meant that Masters were now once more agreeing to work to the Custumary.

At the time that the changes to the oath were made, the Custumary itself was modified. The Steward's pay went up to £30 per year, whilst the Chaplain received £50 a year. They were allowed to live outside the Hospital but not beyond the bounds of the village of St Cross. At each renewal of a lease, but not a copyhold, they both received 6d. in the £1. In place of previous allowances, the Hundred Menne's Hall poor were to get 26s. a year. Brethren were now to have 1s. weekly, plus 12s. for Lent. The barber had his pay increased to 10s. 6d. The present four 'out-brethren' could continue to reside outside the Hospital, but their replacements must always live in. There were also what were called 'sundry trifling differences' to the diet. This new Custumary was to be read on 3 May each year, or on some other convenient date.

Porteus had been Chaplain to the King, and was later to hold the see of Chester whilst still at St Cross. He is remembered for the excellence of his sermons, and for the fact that he extended the graveyard for the brethren into the south-east corner of the grounds around the church. When he was translated to the see of London in 1787 he resigned as Master.

Despite its difficulties, the Hospital retained its high reputation. In 1777, Dr. Samuel Johnson, of dictionary fame, wrote to Bennet Langton on behalf of a friend who had been a painter but could no longer earn a living as he had the palsy. As Langton knew the Bishop of Chester (Porteus), Johnson hoped that he would use his influence for the painter. Warton (Headmaster of Winchester College) had promised his support. He was appealing for a place in St Cross as he did not think he had sufficient pull to win a place at The Chartreux—so at least St Cross came somewhere in the second rank! Unfortunately, his letter does not mention the man's name as presumably the description would be sufficient for Langton, so there is no way of knowing whether Johnson was successful.

There were still ex-service men amongst the brothers. John Hart had been a seaman, involved in the sea wars against Spain. Coming back to his home port of Portsmouth, he bought some damaged planks of a captured Spanish man o' war and made his own coffin from them, as a reminder both of his active days and his eventual end. When he retired to St Cross, he had it hung by a system of pulleys from the ceiling of his room. It was

well decorated with biblical and religious quotations. Every so often, he would haul it down and persuade his visitors to admire it. They thought it a more gruesome reminder of death than he did! Robert Bartholomew was an old soldier of the same wars. He hailed originally from Sherborne and had been present at the capture of Gibraltar in 1704. For many years he had been Porter, in the sense of keeper of the gate (*porta* in Latin), at the Hospital. An oil painting of him is inscribed on the back that he died at the age of 102. Another long-lived brother was Richard Humber, who lived to be 98. Brother John Hockley is mentioned in the register with the note, 'N.B. He dropt down dead just as he was going to dinner'. John Cane was so badly burned whilst baking, at the age of over 80, 'that he expired in extreme pain about fourteen hours after'. Of Robert White, who had been Steward at the Hospital, it is said that 'His funeral was attended by a great number of persons, and at it were given away 9 dozen pairs of gloves, 20 bottles of wine, and one dozen of hatbands'. The 18th-century liking for words

32 *Brother Bartholomew, who served in the siege of Gibraltar and was reputed to be 102 years old.*

which look like Latin is found in the epitaph of Brother Nicholas Knotsford, who died in 1706. He is said to be of '*Hujus Gerontocomny*'! Many vagrants are also listed as buried at St Cross. Presumably they came for the meal and succour it offered, but were too weak really to benefit from it. Mary Oak, one of the few ladies mentioned, is noted as an old maid 'about two feet and a half high'. On a completely different tack, Mary Barling of St Faith's parish did penance in the Chapel of St Cross 'for fornication by her committed'.

That out-brethren flourished in the middle of the century is shown by entries in the brethren's admission register from 1758. In that year, for instance, John Bailey was admitted as 'an in Brother'. The next entry is of William Shuckford in the quaint phrase of 'an Absent Brother'. Four other absent brothers of the time were William Russell, John Crowder, James Eagar, and John Stokes. By 1762, the 'absent brothers' had become 'out brothers' as distinct from the 'in brothers'. A suggestion of long life is made by the fact that only five 'in brothers' were appointed between September 1758 and May 1763.

One thing Porteus had not sworn and that was the oath against simony. This was an essential part of any ecclesiastical appointment. The question to be decided was whether St Cross was to be regarded in that light. The case was put to Sir James Mansfield, and he ruled that the office was probably not ecclesiastical and that a layman might be able to hold it. If it were ecclesiastical, then Porteus had never been Master, because he had not taken the essential oath against simony. In that event, even if he wished to, he could not remain in office. As this question was raised in 1788, just as he moved to the see of London, it had no effect on Porteus. He was no longer Master anyway; but it did have significance in the next century, when the whole question of the rights and duties of Master was under severe scrutiny in the Chancery Courts.

Chapter XI

In Chancery

As the 18th century drew to a close, storm clouds began to gather fiercely around St Cross. By this time, the nomination for Master had passed to the King, George III, who was then just sliding into one of his fits of insanity. He chose John Lockman, and there is a sad irony in the fact that almost twenty years later Lockman, too, should suffer from bouts of insanity. In 1788, he was a canon of Windsor, and had been Clerk of the Chest to George, the Prince of Wales, later George IV.

At first, the Bishop of Winchester, Brownlow North, contested the crown's right to the presentation. George III had claimed it since Porteus had been promoted to a bishopric, in which case customarily the crown could claim the right of presentation. This right depended upon the office actually being ecclesiastical. North claimed that it was lay and took the opinion of three leading lawyers, Sir James Mansfield, Sir William Scott and Lord Erskine. Scott pointed out that the founder was a bishop, that the Charity was later held by a religious body, that nearly all Masters were clergymen, inducted in a religious ceremony, and that it had always been subject to royal presentation, being held *in commendam* or as archbishop's options. He had no doubt that the Mastership was ecclesiastical. Erskine was equally clear that this was a spiritual office, for archbishops could only exercise their option on such posts, and the Master had regularly received the tithes as if he were the incumbent of St Faith. Mansfield disagreed, and pointing to Young, Lisle, Cooke and Shute, suggested that a lay Master was a possibility.

Bishop North accepted Scott's opinion, gave way to the crown and installed Lockman, using words which took on a considerable importance in the next 70 or 80 years:

> We do in due form canonically institute you in the said mastership or Guardianship of the said House or Hospital of St Cross, with the Rectory of St Faith united, and invest you with all and singular appurtenances (you having first before us subscribed the Articles and taken the Oath which are in this case by Law required to be taken and subscribed). And we do by these presents commit unto you the care and government of the souls of the parishioners of the said house or hospital of St Cross, with the rectory of St Faith united; and we do authorise you to preach the word of God in the church of the said house or hospital of St Cross, with the rectory of St Faith united.

It is clear from this that the Bishop now regarded the post as one which included the cure of souls, that it was united with the rectory of St Faith, and so must be ecclesiastical.

Almost as soon as he arrived, Lockman reported the buildings to be in a bad state—scarcely surprising in view of the neglect from which they had suffered. He felt that one of the major problems was dampness, but that there was a cheap way by which this could be solved. According to Lockman's letter to the Bishop, there were only three brethren where the plan had been for 35 brethren and three sisters. He was reverting to Beaufort and ignoring de Blois. This, he claimed, had been the case for more than two hundred and fifty years, since Legh's visitation. 'There are a great number of uninhabited apartments on the fourth side of the courtyard of the said house or hospital which extend from the church about 70 feet.' They were in ruins and useless. Lockman's solution was simple. Pull these buildings down and let light and air into the quadrangle. All would then be well. The Bishop agreed. Accordingly, in 1789 the southern rooms were demolished, leaving quarters only on the west side of the square. Fortunately, he did not realise that there was a faculty already given for the demolition of the east side, or no doubt he would have done that also, to let in even more light and air.

Perhaps another sign of the dilapidation of the buildings was the fact that the statue of the Virgin Mary, on the southern side of Beaufort's Tower, fell down, almost hitting one of the elderly brethren as it dropped to the ground. It had survived Lisle's attack, helped by the intercession of the brethren, but showed total ingratitude in frightening the descendant of its defenders almost to death.

For more than two hundred years an-

33 *Modern statue of the Virgin Mary, replacing the earlier one which fell down in the 18th century.*

other fact of life and death had existed. Over that time, the Roman Catholics had been allowed to bury their dead in St James' churchyard, although the ownership of the land remained firmly with St Cross. In 1800, Lockman sold the land, to the extent of about half an acre, for £41, so that the Catholic Church now owned it. The money received was used to pay off the Land Tax.

34   *The triptych bought by Lockman.*

Lockman also brought the Hospital one of its treasures. For £20 he bought a triptych, painted on oak panels, which now hangs in the Lady Chapel, though it had previously been kept in the Brethren's Hall. Its title is given as *The Rest on the Flight into Egypt*. The centre panel depicts the Virgin Mary, sitting with the baby Jesus on her knee. Her left hand reaches out to grasp some grapes from a plate held by an angel. The plate also has some cherries on it. To her right, Joseph offers a pear. Behind is a landscape, with angels ascending. On the table before her is a pomegranate, an apple and an open book. The symbolism throughout is rife. Grapes represent the wine of the Eucharist and hence the sacrifice of Christ, cherries were regarded as fruits of paradise and represent Heaven. Pomegranates symbolise resurrection. Apples were traditionally the fruit of the tree of knowledge in the Garden of Eden. The open book shows Mary as the Mother of Wisdom. This symbolism is typical of the 16th century, and helps to place the date of the painting as somewhere about 1520. On either side, in the two 'doors' of the triptych, is a saint. To Mary's left is Saint Barbara, recognised by the feather over her shoulder, alluding to the story that, when her father beat her, angels changed the scourges into peacock feathers. In the background is a tower, in which she was believed to have been imprisoned. St Katharine is to the right, holding the sword by which she was beheaded. At first, the paintings were attributed successively to Dürer and Mabuse, who produced similar altar pieces. A triptych entitled *Holy Family Resting on the Flight into Egypt* (now on loan to the Cathedral from St Michael's, Basingstoke) has almost exactly the same central panel and is attributed to Peter Coecke van Aelst of *c*.1530. The St Cross piece could either be a copy, or by the same painter, or from the same school. The painting in the Hospital, dated *c*.1520, is often attributed to the unknown Master of 1518.

Lockman was not above turning the Charity's amenities to his own financial benefit. He could live in great comfort at Windsor, so the Master's lodge was often empty. He therefore let it to the Speaker of the House of Commons, Charles Wolfran Cornwall. There was thus an absentee Master, and a stranger living within the gates—a position which needed an Act of Parliament to end it in 1567. It is paradoxical that the stranger defying such an Act should be the Speaker. As the St Cross register remarked, Cornwall lived at St Cross during parliamentary recesses 'as his former residence at Barton Priors was too small for his retinue, since his advancement to the chair'. He died whilst still in office, a fact which is advertised by the presence of the mace on his somewhat opulent wall memorial in the south aisle. He and his wife were buried in the nave, their resting places being marked by inconspicuous squares of marble carved 'C.W.C.' and 'E.C.'.

Lockman felt that the Custumary gave him wide powers and, because their appointments were totally at the discretion of the Master, that the Chaplain and Steward were his personal servants. He was soon at odds with both, and decided to find out exactly what his rights were. In consequence, he sent the Custumary and other documents to Sir William Wynne asking for legal advice. Wynne wrote back saying that he felt the Custumary was valueless and could not be upheld in court. He agreed that the Steward might be the Master's servant, but said that he must be paid directly from the Master's pocket and not using the Hospital's funds. On the other hand, the Chaplain could not be dismissed without having first had the chance to make his case before the bishop, as his office seemed to be an ecclesiastical benefice. Wynne also stated categorically that the use of Charity funds by the Master was 'a total perversion of the money'. He strongly advised putting the whole matter before the Court of Chancery to get a decree as to how the funds should be administered. Lockman disagreed and wrote to Wynne in October 1792, again using the Custumary as his ground, explaining that he still felt justified in his actions. Wynne repeated his comments, and warned of serious consequences if the Court of Chancery were not approached. He suggested that the letting out of the property in the current manner was probably illegal. This method consisted of letting properties, often for a number of lives, and taking fines, based on the full rental values from the new tenants—fines which the Master, Chaplain, Stewards and brethren (but chiefly the Master) pocketed. Moreover 'by continuing to apply the rents and emoluments of the charity to purposes which none can extenuate in those who are clearly Trustees for the benefit of others, incapable of remonstrating against such injustice', was morally and probably legally wrong. He felt that the whole proceedings smacked of fraud. Lockman took no notice, ignored the advice, and carried on as before. Had he only acted voluntarily on Wynne's letters, the troubles of the next mastership and the expensive legal action which resulted would have been avoided. Indeed, it is just possible that the man who succeeded him as Master would never have done so.

Bishop Brownlow North was obviously not greatly enamoured of Winchester as he and his wife spent much of their time in salubrious watering holes on the continent. On the other hand, he was very keen to ensure that church preferment was kept within the family. His son, Francis, already held four livings and a prebendal stall which produced an income of over £4,500 per annum when, on Lockman's death, the office of Master of St Cross became available. This was an important and wealthy post, so North wished to grant it to his son. Parliament had passed Acts against pluralism in 1802 and 1808, without much effect, but there was no doubt that the church-going public generally resented priests who persisted in holding in plurality. There might thus be opposition to adding the mastership of St Cross to Francis's already long list of benefices.

Bishop North was not worried about nepotism, but did feel a little bit chary of inflicting too much and too obvious pluralism on his diocese. If the office at the Hospital could now be regarded as a lay one, then the argument against pluralism might not be raised, as no one had hitherto objected to Francis's other collection of livings. He therefore decided to use a slightly different form of words at the institution of his son, rather than those he had used 20 years previously at Lockman's collation:

> We do hereby freely, and of our mere good will, give and confer on you the Office of Master or Guardian of the House or Hospital of St Cross, and we do in due form canonically institute you in and to the said office of Master or Guardian of the said House or Hospital of St Cross and invest you with all and singular the rights members and or appurtenances belonging thereunto (you having before us subscribed the Articles and taken the oaths and made or subscribed the Declaration which at this case are by law to be taken made and subscribed). And we do by these presents commit unto you the care and government of the said house or hospital, as far as the same belongeth or appertaineth to the said Office of Master or Guardian.

At no time was St Faith mentioned, nor was there any suggestion that his office carried with it a cure of souls. Perhaps just as significant was the fact that Francis North, according to the Bishop's Registry, read himself in to office on Sunday 10 January 1808, Sunday being the usual day for ecclesiastical appointments. This at least suggested that there might be some lingering doubts about on which side of the fence St Cross lay. Bishop North had now moved over into the ranks of those accepting the post as a lay one, even if it happened to be held by a cleric. This way, the appointment of his son would perhaps not raise too much opposition.

Like all the Masters, officers and brethren, at least since 1696, Francis North had to swear to obey all the customs and usages of St Cross. Effectually, this meant that he was to take the Custumary as his guide and work according to its rules. In the mythology of St Cross, North has become the black figure—and, indeed, he did much that was wrong. However, having been installed without cure of souls, and with no voice raised in protest, he was entitled to feel that his office was essentially a lay one. Equally, the Custumary would clearly appear to be the document by which he should organise his life, just as his predecessors had done.

North examined the conditions of the Custumary carefully and at once made a number of improvements in their terms. He added £6 5s. to the annual pay of the brethren, and himself paid for a doctor to attend to them when sick. Each brother was

35 *Meal-time in the Brethren's Hall during the 19th century.*

given a new gown (valued at 'about £19, including the making') at Christmas. Meals were provided four days a week in the Brethren's Hall, plus provisions to take to their rooms on the other days. The Master gave an extra dinner at Christmas to the brethren and provided '6 bushels of coal'. The Chaplain and Steward both had their stipend raised to £80, although it was not until the Acts of 1813 and 1817 that this figure came to be accepted as the minimum for curates. Additionally, the Chaplain received £15 a year as Minister of the Freefolk Chapel. As North continued to live in Alresford, and only appeared at St Cross on those rent collection days on which he did not send his Steward, he allowed the Chaplain, Rev. W.T. Williams, to live in the Master's house rent free. Williams had to pay for the use of the garden and, although it is normally said that he was charged £16 per annum for the privilege, the Hospital accounts show a figure of £8. The Hundred Menne's Hall poor, having varied in number through the ages from 100 to

200 to 40, was now set at 20. Because the local poor did not think it worth walking out to St Cross for 6d. a week, the money was doubled to 1s. a week, commensurate with the reduction in numbers. The Wayfarers' Dole consisted of two loaves of about twenty ounces each, cut into 12 pieces, hence providing for 24 travellers. Each piece of bread was accompanied by a horn of beer containing just less than half a pint. There were also for brothers, Chaplain and Steward a share in the fines paid at the renewal of leases. As Lockman had suffered from dementia at the end of his time in office, and had not dealt with leases at all, there were a large number due to be renewed at the start of North's reign. As a result, all involved gained a considerable amount in shares of fines, though, of course, North benefited most. The custom of leasing out land for lives meant that the renewals otherwise only occurred infrequently. One plot of land was let for three lives, the youngest being just 16, and so likely to live 50 years longer at least, thus guaranteeing a fixed rent to the lessee for that period. Many of the rents were at levels which had been set in the 16th century. North did at least increase some, to the benefit of the Hospital, whilst he gained from the large amounts paid by lessees in order to obtain renewals. He also spent money on maintaining the brethren's quarters. At least £6,000 was said to have been spent between 1808 and 1836, in marked contrast to what had been done by many previous Masters. Nor did he neglect his outside duties. In 1849, the *Hampshire Chronicle* reported that three cottages in Alresford had been destroyed by fire and that the Master, who was rector of the parish, had been generous with his aid.

North continued to insist that his office was a lay one. When he was asked to complete some forms for the archdeacon's visitation (how modern this sounds!), as all incumbents were expected to do, he wrote back that presumably the forms had been sent to him in error. His post was not an ecclesiastical benefice, he was merely guardian, the church was the chapel to the Hospital, and he was in no way subject to ecclesiastical jurisdiction or residence. He had a chance to make the point again in the following year when he wrote, 'I am not incumbent of St Faith's; have nothing to do with its officers or parochial arrangements'. The next year he stated categorically that he held no clerical office in the Hospital.

Although interested in St Cross primarily as a source of income, North also watched events there. A letter he wrote in 1829 made it clear that he expected the brothers to observe strictly all the customs and rules of the Foundation. Brother Forder was warned that he must never again appear with a working apron under his gown. Moreover, he was no longer to use a workshop in the Beaufort Tower for which he had no permission. The Master's own position was to be remembered. Whenever he arrived, however unexpect- edly, it was the Porter's duty to stand at the door of his lodge with all his staff, and to be there again as the Master left.

In 1837, the Charity Commissioners made a report on St Cross. Basically, they drew attention to the custom of fines and leasing by lives. They pointed out that taking a fine of two years' rent for a lease of one life, eight years for two lives and 16 years for three lives encouraged letting at a multiple of lives, which was to the disadvantage of the Hospital, though a source of profit at the time for those who shared the fines. The more lives involved and hence the likelihood of a long lease, the greater the profit. However, their report supported North in his actions and found nothing illegal in what he was doing, as he had worked within the Custumary, which appeared to be the guiding document for the Hospital. By then, incidentally, North had succeeded to his cousin's title of Earl of Guilford, inheriting also two estates whose value was computed at £18,000 per annum. He thereupon gave up his prebendal stall in Winchester Cathedral and the stipend of £1,000 that went with it, but retained all other benefices, including, of course, St Cross.

One visitor of the time was John Keats. St Cross insists that he wrote *Ode to Autumn* whilst sitting in the grounds. Certainly he frequently walked out across the meadows when he was staying in Winchester. In a letter, he wrote, 'I arrive, that is my worship arrives, at the foundation of St Cross, which is a very interesting old place, both for its Gothic tower and alms square, and for the appropriation of its rich rents to a relation of the Bishop of Winchester'. Guilford's peculation was obviously known to outsiders from the 1820s but no one did anything about it, as it was the norm for the Charity, and the brethren and buildings showed no sign of suffering from neglect.

Gradually, interest was aroused in the method of renting out the properties belonging to the Hospital. In the 1840s, the *Hants Independent* printed an article about St Cross:

> St. Cross Hospital, Winchester. A large property is now become finable by the master and brethren of this hospital. The fine paid, or to be paid, is nearly £13,000, the whole of which is paid to the master and brethren for the time being, the master getting no less than £10,706 for his share of the spoil! It is said that this valuable property consists of the great tithes of Crondal and other parishes, and is of the value of upwards of £2,000 per annum. By the mode of management now existing at St Cross Hospital, it will thus be seen that a property belonging to it, and worth two thousand pounds a year, is comparatively worthless to the charity, and totally diverted from the purposes of the donors of the property—the relief and maintenance of the poor and destitute. The whole and only portion of this splendid property (as well as many others equally valuable) that goes towards the maintenance of the charitable foundation of which it is an endowment, is some paltry quit rent, it may be, of some five or six pounds a year, the real income of it being transferred by the process of fines into the pocket of the master for the time being.

The article goes on to comment on other properties which would produce fines for the Master, but little rent for the Hospital. If only the rents were at the proper level, the Hospital would have an income of about £4,000 more. The expenses of the Hospital were only £1,000, so that the Charity could actually maintain four times the number of brethren—and this only looked at a proportion of the lands and tithes held by St Cross. National papers, such as *The Times, The Globe, Morning Herald, Morning Chronicle,* and *Morning Post* took up the story. For a while, the nonconformists found in the misuse of funds by a clergyman, and a noble clergyman at that, a stick to beat the Established Church with, but they soon lost interest, as did the press.

At about the same time, Rev. Henry Holloway retired to live in the parish of St Faith. He had held parish livings and had been, in fact, a pluralist. Thus, it was not on this ground that he took issue with Guilford. The Hospital Chaplain, Rev. Williams, was far too busy administering to the needs of the brethren to deal much with any matters from St Faith. Parishioners paid tithes of about £260 per annum to St Cross, and Holloway felt that they were simply not getting any value for their money. Worse still, Guilford, who received the tithes, claimed that he was not rector of the parish and had no duties there. Apparently, then, St Faith had no church, no churchwardens, and no priest. As an articulate man, he wrote a series of letters to the newspapers, fulminating against Guilford.

He was not alone in feeling that Guilford was capable of misuse of tithes. Rev. R. Lewin was the curate at Yately, one of the St Cross livings—a post he held for almost forty years. He wrote:

> The tithes of Yately, which at this time amount to £570 per annum, and which have exceeded that sum, are let by the master of St Cross upon lives. My own receipt from the lessee during the term of my incumbency has been £24 per annum, minus a small deduction from that magnanimous amount, on account of tithes.
> The tithes are taken away annually by the agent of the lessee.
> Excepting in one instance, I have never received from them toward the relief of the parochial poor one farthing. Upon that occasion I received from the lessee £2 at the time of the potato disease.
> I have, I think, during the period of my incumbency, upon two occasions, and upon two occasions only, applied for aid in behalf of the parochial poor to the present master of St Cross—in one case, for one guinea per year toward the support of a Sunday School; and in the other, in the case of the potato disease—in both cases without success.
> His refusal in the second case was contained in a letter, as to style, haughty and absurd; as to matter, ungenerous and unchristian.
> The said Rev. the Earl of Guilford has received from this parish, in fines, many thousand pounds.

The letter highlights the weakness of the fines system, from the point of view of the parish. As far as the Master, or any other tithe owner throughout the land, was concerned, he had carried out a business transaction, selling the tithes for a period of time to someone else. He had no responsibility, therefore, for how the tithes were spent. The lessee also bought a business opportunity, and was not likely to return much money to the parish, in view of the large lump sum he had paid in fines for the privilege of owning the tithes. He had to get what amounted to at least the proper interest rates on his money as well as some repayment of capital.

At length, in 1849, Joseph Hume, a radical M.P., took up the case in parliament. Russell's government of the time was under pressure over reforms to the Poor Law, Health, and a strengthening of the Ten Hours Bill (for a working day no longer than ten hours!). The Radicals, on the left of politics, were happy to seize on any problem to attack the ruling classes. Hume introduced a resolution asking that the Queen should set up an inquiry into the revenues of St Cross, and the duties and emoluments of the Master, so that parliament might then proceed to place the Hospital on a proper footing. The Commons passed the resolution, and the Attorney-General told Guilford that an information had been filed. There were 16 heads to the prayer and they ranged through an examination of the properties held and lost by St Cross, the system of fines, misuse of the funds of the Hospital and maladministration.

Guilford replied that he presumed the information was laid out of jealousy as he had just received a large fine. In fact, this was £10,706 mentioned in the *Hants Independent* for Crondal. 'In my 77th. year I wish only for peace, and have to complain, not of the invasion of my vested rights, but of repeated inquisitions after having been publicly acquitted of all malversion.' There was some justice in these remarks, as the Charity Commissioners' Report of 1837 had made it clear that his acts were not illegal. 'I wish therefore to be freed from the expence of a Suit in Chancery to the injury of my family, and to resign my office which I find obnoxious to calumny and persecution.'

Bishop North had been succeeded by Bishop Sumner, who was the only man who could accept Guilford's resignation; but he was determined that the whole matter should now be thrashed out. Anxious to avoid the usual long Chancery case, Guilford began to rethink his position. For years he had been stating that his office was totally lay. Now he wrote, 'The mastership is an ecclesiastical benefice, to which I was instituted and inducted, and read in, in the church'. The advantage of this to him would be that he was answerable only to the Bishop, and that the Courts of Chancery would have no power over him. However, it was rapidly decided that Chancery should continue with the case, which revolved largely around the question of the Master's rights and duties, and was mainly a question as to the mismanagement of affairs by Guilford.

For his part, Guilford now felt that he would be better off on his estates rather than holding any church benefices. Accordingly, in 1850, he resigned from Old Alresford, New Alresford, Medstead and St Mary's, Southampton. These resignations were all accepted by the Bishop. His refusal to allow Guilford to give up the Mastership of St Cross stresses his determination to get this matter settled once and for all. There was apparently a 'quid pro quo' suggested to the Master. Writing in 1850 to Rev. Holloway, a friend of the earl said that Holloway's continued campaign to find evidence against the Master in the hopes of getting repayment of the fines taken would be a breach of faith. 'His Lordship was given to understand that by the resignation of his preferments no further proceedings would be taken against him relative to St Cross.' It was a vain hope, and the case dragged on.

When he left Alresford, Guilford had a sale of his unwanted possessions. The *Hampshire Chronicle* recorded, amongst other items, 15 four-poster beds, 62 dozen choice old Port, Claret, Madeira, Sherry, Champagne, Hock and other wines, plus two butts of fine ale. One hopes that the 62 dozen refers to the total of all bottles rather than each individual wine. People of the time must have wondered at what went on in Alresford that required 15 four-poster beds.

The Chaplain, Rev. Williams, died in 1850, whilst Guilford still had the nomination to that office. As he had just given up Alresford, he was afraid that his curate might not be retained by the new rector. Accordingly, he presented Rev. Archibald Neil Campbell Maclachlan, the curate, to the office of Chaplain at St Cross.

By 1853, all the evidence had been collected and the various documents, going back to 1137, copied in fine copper plate for the barristers. One point was certainly made clear. Whatever else Mrs. Wright may have done, she did not destroy all documents, but perhaps only those which she felt might incriminate her husband, for a huge pile of original papers was produced.

Since the 'Consuetudinarium' or Custumary depended upon the fact that it showed the customs to be followed in the absence of other guidance, the existence of all these documents made the Custumary, as the Attorney-General put it, 'one of the most extraordinary documents that was ever produced and relied upon in a Court of Justice'. He went on, 'A more barefaced and shameless document than this "Consuetudinarium" could not well, in my opinion, have been framed, nor could a more manifest and probably wilful breach of trust have been committed by the Master and Brethren ... Since that time, to the filing of this information, the Hospital has continued to be carried on, according to this glaring and (as I think) discreditable breach of trust.' He stated that the Hospital must be regarded as a lay foundation, and that the position of the Bishop of Winchester as Visitor in no way prevented the case from being brought into Chancery. He made an injunction restraining any grant of leases on fines, set on foot an inquiry into the present leases, and demanded a scheme to settle the affairs of the Charity. Guilford was ordered to repay any fines, rents, or profits which were received after the date of the information, and he had to pay for any necessary repairs from that date. It was accepted that he had been canonically instituted into the Mastership. It was made clear that the court could appoint a receiver to manage the trust property, and, in the event, did so. There was no union between the church of St Cross, which was a private chapel, and the living of St Faith. The Attorney-General was not even sure if there could be a parish of St Faith since the church had been pulled down in 1507, and so, if there really were no church, it was unlikely that there could legally be any churchwarden.

The new scheme was only to go into operation when the Earl was no longer Master. He had been anxious to resign since 1849. He was now told by the Bishop that his resignation would be accepted once he had paid for repairs to the extent of £2,587 and had repaid fines and rents totalling £1,107 18s. 8d. Two years later, in 1855, he had complied completely, and was allowed to retire from office, and live out the rest of his life on his family estates.

Holloway was not entirely pleased with the result of his grand endeavour. One question, to him perhaps the most important, had not been addressed in the judgement. In no way had the position of the parish of St Faith been determined. As early as 1851, Holloway had obtained a 'mandamus' for the election of churchwardens at St Faith. He thus ensured the calling of a parish meeting. At this meeting, he himself was not elected, but was chosen in 1853. One of his plans was that he would obtain £6,000 from the £9,000 in tithes that he estimated Guilford had received, and erect a parish church and school. After all, there was no parish church building. It was only by consent that the church of St Cross could be used. Again and again, he wrote letters to the press. He told parishioners that if Guilford were not properly rector of St Faith's, then all the marriages celebrated since 1808 were illegal. He tried to get the people not to pay any tithes to St Cross. The 1853 decision seemed to Holloway to be both weak and unsound. He decided to take action.

In May 1854, the Chaplain, Rev. Maclachlan, was absent from Winchester. Woolridge, the Steward, went to the church of St Cross to oversee its opening. His letter, as quoted by Lord Guilford's solicitors, explains what happened.

> In compliance with my instructions not to take any other notice of Mr. Holloway's acts whatever they may be today other than to be present and take Minutes of his proceedings, I attended at St Cross this morning for that purpose and I will now give you an account of what took place.

My son and myself were in the Court at ten o'clock where we found Mr. Holloway and Mr. Andrews and some others standing near the Church door. At the usual time 1/4 past 10, the Porter unlocked the doors and Holloway stood near evidently on the watch as to what my actions were to be. I did not go near him and about 20 minutes past 10 I left the Porter's Lodge and went down the Cloisters to enter the Church by the side door. Holloway saw me and before I got into the Church he went in at the large door and I found him standing in the Passage guarding the entrance to the reading desk. My son and I took our seat close to the reading desk on the opposite side of the passage and when we were seated Holloway went up to the Communion Table where the Bread and Wine for the sacrament was covered over with a Cloth as usual, raised the Cloth, saw of course the Bread and Wine, covered it up again and came back resuming his guard at the reading desk door so that no one could enter it without his getting out of the way—he remained thus until Revd. Mr. Crockett (who does duty in Mr. Maclachlan's absence) came into the Church as usual and when he came to the reading desk Mr. Holloway said he must request him to produce his Licence from the Bishop authorising him to act as Curate of the Parish. Mr. Crockett told him he had no such Licence but that he had a Letter from the Bishop authorising him to do all the duty during the Revd. Mr. Maclachlan's absence which that gentle-man did when he was present or to that effect. Mr. Holloway said he was aware of that as he had written to the Bishop who had declined to interfere. Upon this Mr. Holloway took a paper from his pocket or having it in his hand opened it and having then gone into the reading desk he shut the door and commenced reading from this paper which was to the effect that by Statute and Crown Law he as Churchwarden of the Parish of St Faith with the Parish of Holy Cross united, of which the church was the Parish Church, he was justified in not allowing any one to do duty there who could not and did not produce the proper authority from the Bishop authorising him so to do. The paper, as I understood it as he appeared to be reading what was written, stated that what he did was not personal to Mr. Crockett but done to try the right of Lord Guilford to the Church in a Court of Common Law as the Court of Chancery had no jurisdiction.

Mr. Crockett then (standing in the passage and Holloway being in the reading desk) asked him 'Am I to understand that you prevent me from performing the service?'. Holloway said he did and as I was close to Mr. Crockett and wishing no violence or unseemly conduct should take place in the Church, I opened the door of the seat I was in and said 'Come in here Sir'. Mr. Crockett did so and as soon as he was seated, Holloway said there is no one here legally authorised to perform the Service and as it is my duty as Churchwarden to see it is done I shall therefore do it myself. He then immediately commenced the Morning service upon which Mr. Crockett, I and my son and several others left the Church as did also eleven of the Brothers, two only, Tigwell and March staying behind. Holloway went through the whole of the Morning Service and having finished the Communion Service dismissed the Congregation with the usual Prayer and came out of the Church very quickly not staying to administer the sacrament. I waited till he had left the Court and I then gave the Porter instructions to lock up the Church as usual which he did.

What Holloway actually read out in church was:

That in order finally to extinguish the claim of Lord Guilford to the benefice of St Cross Hospital cum St Faith, or to afford him an opportunity to try the question of

his title, I am under the necessity as Churchwarden of the parish to interdict Mr.
Crockett, or any one else as his nominee, from doing any duty whatsoever within the
church, or in any building or place of the hospital or parish, unless both the building
or place with the individual to perform the same were licensed by the Lord Bishop
of the Diocese; for that under any other circumstances both the ministers and the
hearers were liable to the penalties imposed by the act for performing public worship
in unlicensed and unconsecrated places. Under the present circumstances, and for the
above reasons, I interdict you from performing any public worship or parochial duty
(save baptisms in cases of emergency) within the church or parish of St Cross Hospital
and St Faith, or in any building or place within the said united parishes, until specially
licensed by the Lord Bishop of the Diocese.

Holloway himself was not licensed, but as churchwarden could read the services, in
order to provide worship for the congregation, when no other properly qualified person
was available. He went as far as that on the morning of 7 May, but, although he was a
priest, he did not, as Woolridge says, 'administer the sacraments'. This kept him within the
bounds of his complaint against all others.

All this was better than a circus for the inhabitants of the Hospital and village of St
Cross. There were no other entertainments, except what they could provide for themselves
at home. They thus crowded to church on the following Sunday to see the next instal-
ment. Not only was St Cross there in force, but many Wintonians made the walk across
the meadows, in hope of witnessing something exciting. They must have been disap-
pointed, as all went quietly, with Holloway once more reading the service, and the
Rev. Crockett remaining in the background. A few weeks later, the Bishop had obtained
an injunction from the Master of the Rolls against Holloway, forbidding him to interfere
with the services at St Cross. It was held that the church of St Cross had not become the
parish church of St Faith. Consequently, even though Rev. Holloway was churchwarden
of St Faith, he had no right to perform or provide for the performance of divine service
in St Cross, nor did he have any form of authority in the church there.

In the few weeks between the incident in church and the injunction, the *Hampshire
Chronicle* had published what were said to be letters from Holloway, which could be read
as suggesting that he was using underhand means in pursuing a vendetta against Guilford.
By now, Holloway had the bit between his teeth, and took John Jacobs, the paper's
publisher, to court for 'imputing sundry offences' to him. He was victorious, but only
received £2 damages plus his costs. After winning his case, Holloway implicated Lord
Guilford by saying that the earl had given £850 to Jacob to pay for his defence. Possibly
this was true, as no one took up the challenge.

To the locals, Holloway was St George, fighting the dragons of a wicked Master and
the Press. In August, they gave him a reception 'in the pleasure-garden in the rear of the
White Horse Inn'. Although the celebration was local, the Chairman of the day was Mr.
R. Andrews of Southampton. There were a number of speeches, and a band. Andrews said
of Holloway, 'The Reverend Gentleman had freely spent his time and money in order to
protect the institution from one of the grossest robberies, and had gone bravely on in
defiance of the calumniations and libels which had been used to terrify him into silence'.
Better than the speeches, Holloway was given a blue purse full of sovereigns, and an

engraved gold watch, with chain and key. One is led to wonder whether the reports were accurate, and that the 'watch' should have been 'clock', when the words of the engraving are read: 'This watch, a gold chain, and a purse, value £100, were with great respect presented by the working men of Winchester and friends to the Rev. H. Holloway, in consideration of his zealous and untiring efforts to restore the noble privileges and charities of the Hospital of St Cross—trusting that the same disinterested spirit which has hitherto prompted him will shortly make him triumph over the many obstacles that surround his benevolent exertions. August, 1854.' Surely, even a clock would have been hard pushed to carry such an inscription. Perhaps the Mr. R. Andrews who was the Chairman was the Mr. Andrews of the Steward's letter who had stood alongside Holloway in the church.

Holloway replied, and thanked *The Times* and *Daily News* for their help. He claimed that he had received some very deep confessions from a Mr. Lintott, a recently deceased brother of the Hospital. Holloway asserted that the brother had died because 'certain promises and inducements held out to him, in connection with Hospital affairs, had preyed on his mind'.

Although in practical terms, this was the end of the affair, Holloway continued to struggle on, obsessed with the idea of great wrongs done to St Cross. As late as 1861, he petitioned parliament for it to say that there were two charities at St Cross, that all leases made by Guilford should be null and void, and that an Act should be passed to legalise all marriages, etc., performed in the church of St Cross for centuries. In the course of his petition, he claimed that if all the rents were restored to St Cross, the revenue 'will maintain about four hundred crippled soldiers and sailors permanently, instead of now only thirteen men'. His figures were grossly out of proportion, and parliament rejected the petition. Holloway continued to fulminate, not always against Guilford, but never attained his perfect objective. Even at the end, he would have regarded it as unjust that he died before his *bête noire*, who continued to enjoy his country estates for some years after the end of the case.

All this had considerable effects upon law and literature. The mid-19th century produced several examples of misuse of Charity funds, of which St Cross seemed to be but the largest and longest-running. Parliament decided to attack the abuse by introducing new laws. When the Charitable Trusts Act was being debated, the *Daily News* wrote that it could not see how there could be any further debate in view of the St Cross judgement. In time, the Act was passed, extending the powers of the Charity Commissioners to enforce the proper administration of any charity, be it lay or ecclesiastical. The fact that the St Cross story had revolved largely around the question of whether the Master was a lay office or an ecclesiastical one, and the fact that an ecclesiastical charity might avoid the law courts, had not been missed.

Trollope's *The Warden* was written in the year 1852-1853 when the papers were full of the St Cross case. Whilst he was at Winchester College, Trollope must surely have learned of St Cross and had some idea of its state under Guilford. His description of the approach to Hiram's Hospital could be read as directions to St Cross. Trollope's hospital stands near the banks of a river which flows to the Cathedral close, and is approached down a road from the London road and through a heavy gateway in a large stone arch. There is even a broad gravel walk. The name of the present approach to St Cross Hospital is 'The Gravels', tarmac though it is. Trollope himself says that his story is based on a case and letters he had read in *The Times*, where the St Cross case and Holloway's letters received their fair share of prominence. In the novel, there are at least 12 mentions of Lord Guilford and St Cross by name. They are first mentioned as early as Chapter Two. Mr. Harding is made to think about the case and feel concern, really about the pressures brought to bear on people by the press, although the wrongs committed were also in mind. 'He had read with pity, amounting almost to horror, the strictures which had appeared from time to time against Earl Guilford as Master of St Cross, and the invectives that had been heaped on rich diocesan dignitaries and overgrown sinecure pluralists.' There can be no doubt that Trollope had St Cross in mind, and it is to this institution that we owe the splendid literary invention of Barchester.

CHAPTER XII

Aftermath

A man of considerable ability and determination was required as Master, both to clear up after the case and, to a lesser degree, deal with the well-meant interference of Holloway. Such a man was fortunately found in the Rev. Lewis Macnaughtan Humbert. It is worthy of note, in view of the energetic and great work he did, that he was over 65 when he was collated. He took the normal oaths of allegiance to the Queen, rejected the Pope and all foreign powers, promised he had not obtained the post through simony and agreed to 'faithfully observe all the statutes, ordinances, and customs' of St Cross.

Perhaps the most important part lay in the Bishop's next few phrases. 'And we do, by these presents, commit unto you the cure, government, and administration of the said House or Hospital: saving always to ourselves our episcopal rights, and the dignity and honour of our Cathedral Church of Winchester.' No one should doubt the rights of the Bishop over the church and Master. However, there was no word of St Faith in this collation but the use of the word 'cure' showed that the position of Master was to be regarded as ecclesiastical.

At the end of the Chancery case, St Cross was placed under a Receiver, responsible to the courts, so that the financial problems, caused not least by the heavy bills of lawyers, could be settled alongside the normal day-to-day expenses. The man appointed was John Gill Comely, who was later to be employed by St Cross in the same capacity, but then responsible only to the Trustees. The Trustees were an important feature of the new scheme for running the Hospital, and met for the first time in April 1857.

36 *Rev. L.M. Humbert, the first Master appointed under the 1857 scheme.*

117

The first scheme for regulating the Charity was drawn up by the Charity Commissioners in June 1855, but by 1900 had been varied in minor details in 1857, 1858, 1874, 1875, 1878, 1881, and 1898. Despite the frequent changes, there was now a regular, legal framework within which the Hospital should work. All the 15 trustees were to be members of the Church of England, with the *ex officio* members being the Master, the Dean of Winchester, the Mayor, the Warden of Winchester College, a member of Winchester Town Council, and the rector of Compton. The other original trustees were: Dr. Crawford, Major Lowth, Mr. Waddington, W. Barrow Simonds, M.P., Mr. Benny, Sir F. Baring, Sir William Heathcote, Viscount Eversley, Lord Northbrook. The various schemes kept a close control over major expenditure and investment, and ensured that the brethren and buildings were both properly looked after. At first, the Master's salary was fixed at £250 per annum, but was increased over the years to £250 plus £250 that could be withheld if the duties were done unsatisfactorily, and up to £100 to 'be applied by him towards providing a salary for any Assistant Minister or Curate who may be employed to assist the Master in the discharge of his duties in relation to the Church of St Cross and the Parish of St Faith, provided that any such Assistant Minister shall be on the footing of a Licensed Curate in and for the Parish of St Faith, and shall be subject to all the incidents of that position'. It may be noted that the query over licensing was the basis of Holloway's complaint in 1861.

Although not specifically mentioned in the collation, St Faith's position was made perfectly clear in the Scheme. The Master

> shall also perform, with reference to the parishioners and inhabitants of the parish of St Faith, in the churchyard and elsewhere in the said Parish, all the usual duties of an Incumbent towards the parishioners and inhabitants of his parish, and shall not be entitled to take any fees from any of the inmates, parishioners and inhabitants. He shall keep the Registers of Baptisms, Burials and Marriages, and shall transmit copies of the same in such manner as Incumbents of parishes are required by law to do.

Thus, the long argument about the status of the Master was now finally ended.

Within the church, priority in seating was to be given to 'the inmates of the Hospital', with parishioners of St Faith having second call on all seats, which were to be free. The brothers, in fact, were soon given their own stalls in the choir area of the church. After the revival of the Red Brethren in 1881, there were once more two classes of brothers, the brethren of the Hospital of St Cross (often called the Original Foundation or Black Brothers) and the brethren of the Almshouse of Noble Poverty (called Red or Beaufort Brothers), with a proviso that there should never be less than 13 brethren of the Hospital foundation, with a maximum of 18. The Noble Poverty brethren were restricted to a total of nine. 'The Brethren on the Foundation of the Hospital of St Cross shall be poor men who shall have attained the age of fifty years at the least, who shall not have been in receipt of parochial relief within twelve months next preceding the time of election, and who shall be so reduced in strength as not to be able to work.' This was a slight variation from de Blois' original conditions, in that his men had only to be weak and unable to look after themselves, but not necessarily poor—though in practice they always were. 'The Brethren on the Foundation of the Almshouse of Noble Poverty shall

37 *Minute of guidance sent to all Trustees prior to their first meeting in April 1857.*

be poor men who shall have attained the age of fifty years at the least, who shall not have been in receipt of parochial relief within twelve months next preceding the time of the election, and who shall have been reduced by misfortune from independence to poverty.' The age limit was later raised to 65 for the Hospital foundation and 60 for the Noble Poverty group.

Instead of providing food and drink for poor people at the gate, the Trustees now arranged for 27 single pensioners, men or women, who were over 65 and not strong enough to work, to receive 8s. a week, plus 18 married couples at 10s. a week, on the Hospital foundation. From the Noble Poverty foundation, on the same conditions as of the Hospital foundation, there were four pensions of £40 per year for married couples and nine of 10s. a week for single people.

Detailed instructions were laid down as to the duties of Trustees, Master, Clerk, Receiver, Porter, the methods of election of brothers and pensioners, the places in which money could be invested, and how leases were to be signed. Any questions were to be addressed to the Charity Commissioners. Gone were the days when the Master could regard himself as lord and master of all he surveyed.

A major problem facing the Trustees was the state of repair of the buildings. As their advisor and architect, they chose William Butterfield, who had already some experience in both designing and restoring churches. In 1857, he was at work on Winchester College, and thus knew some of St Cross' problems by repute. He remained architect to the Trustees until 1893. The object of Butterfield's work was to restore the church to its original repaired state. Much of the outside had been covered with plaster at some stage and this was all removed, revealing the stone and flint exterior. Inside the building, he attempted as little change as possible. His report to the Trustees in April 1858 read: 'Internally, the Church is very damp; and it will never be otherwise until its pavements and floors have been taken up and the soil below excavated and removed. The walls and piers generally require to be carefully cleansed from whitewash, and the stone and purbeck marble to be everywhere exposed, and repaired where they have been cut away. There is dry rot in some of the wooden floors. It is quite undesirable to spend money upon a repair of the present arrangements. A general refitting is very desirable.'

Taking their duties very seriously, the Trustees also interviewed separately each brother resident in 1857, all of whom expressed themselves satisfied 'since their pay had been increased'. 'Accommodation for the parish was stated to be insufficient and the partitions in the body of the Church are not convenient and very injurious to the beauty of the building.' There were places both in the church and the Beaufort Tower where the rain got in. It was felt that the open charcoal fire in the middle of the Brethren's Hall was 'disagreeable and can scarce be wholesome'. Several brothers seemed to have visitors staying, some of whom were perhaps paying the brother concerned—and, in any case, visitors should not be permitted to stay overnight, 'except in the case of wives'. It is interesting that wives might be categorised as overnight visitors! A library or common room for the brethren should be provided, as a 'comfort to them' with the provision of 'even a Weekly Newspaper'.

These were not the most encouraging reports for the Trustees to read, as the almost £6,000 owed after the Chancery Court case was a financial millstone tied around their necks, and most of the reported comments would cost money to implement. It was estimated that the rents of the Hospital property should amount to about £9,000, but that the actual receipts were in the region of £1,700. This was because so many were let out on lives at a very low rent. Fordingbridge Farm, for example, was worth £72 p.a. but was let out at two lives (one of age 82 and the second of 80) at £1 12s. Two houses in St Cross were valued at £58 and were let to James Randall for 16s. on one life of sixty-nine. The Parsonage at Whitchurch should have fetched £1,608 p.a. but Mr. Portal held it on one life of 46 for £353. The only bright feature was that estimated expenditure was £1,450, so that there ought to be a surplus of some £250.

Rev. Humbert set about raising funds by many means. The Wandering Minstrels were persuaded to give several concerts, by which over £100 was raised. Mr. Portal offered £50 'if nine other persons will contribute a like sum for the same purpose within the present month'. Humbert advertised in the *Hampshire Chronicle* of 25 November, listing the names of Dowager Viscountess Gort, Melville Portal, Sir William Heathcote, Sir J.C. Jervoise, Sir Henry St John Mildmay, Charles Buxton, 'A curate in Hampshire, not a native', and a 'County Neighbour' as having answered the call. 'As the specified time is now nearly expired, and two more contributors are still required, any persons (Natives or not) who are willing to contribute £50 are requested to communicate their intention, without delay, to the Rev. L.M. Humbert, Master of St Cross.' The appeal was successful and three more contributors were won. During Rev. Humbert's last year in office, 1868, the first of what has become a great feature of St Cross life, the annual fête, was held. On the back of the sheet advertising it, Lord Heathcote has written, 'Sent 10s. in stamps'. Other supporters noted are the Countess of Portsmouth from Devon, Lady Charlotte Portal of Micheldever Station, Hon. Miss Lefevre, Winchfield, Lady Bycroft, Basingstoke, Mr. Henry Garnier, Deanery, Winchester, Mr. Simmonds, Abbott's Barton, Julian Yonge, Otterbourne, Alfred Barton, Bishopstoke, Lady Heathcote, Hursley Park. It will be seen from this list that the area of appeal was widespread, and even beyond Hampshire.

One way and another, when added to what could be provided from general Hospital funds, enough money was raised to enable restoration work to commence. A noted local antiquarian, F.J. Baigent, came to look at the work in progress and suggested that the two octagonal pillars in the choir, which dated from 1387, were merely casings around something else. When a few outer stones were removed, some flint work was exposed. Going further into the column, some much smaller Purbeck marble columns were found. Baigent deduced that these were columns from the 12th century, probably about 1160, and were later encased for strengthening in about 1165. Butterfield reshaped the octagonal piers, making them rectangular, and inserted a total of eight Derbyshire marble pillars at the four corners. Some of the original Purbeck marble, dating from the 12th century, can still be seen at the base of the central piers in the choir. In his examination of the columns, Butterfield was able to say that the folded palm-leaf decorations on the capitals in the north-east corner of the clerestory identified them as being the work of a Spanish mason who later also worked at Winchfield. It is a tribute to the importance and wealth of 12th-century St Cross that it was able to attract a worker from so great a distance.

The two eastern windows which had been filled in were now reopened. All the abundant whitewash on the church walls was slowly removed, and replaced with the

38 *Advertisement for the first St Cross fête, held in 1868 and still an important annual event.*

designs and colours Butterfield maintained had been present originally. *The Builder* in 1865 reported the colours used: deep red, white, bluish slate, Indian Red, pale carnation, bluish grey, subdued green, black, and gold. All the painted designs have since been removed, but the description suggests a very garish interior, quite unlike modern and Victorian taste. However, it is certainly true that Norman churches were far brighter than their present-day descendants, and it is quite possible that Butterfield's decorations were close to the original. The altar rails were also made to Butterfield's design from wrought iron, with the curled parts picked out in gold. They were given to the church by Major and Mrs. South.

One important feature was still missing. The Master pointed out that there was no satisfactory pulpit, as the old one was in a very poor state of repair. He was able to persuade Mr. W.A. Savage to give the money for a new one, in memory of his daughter, Leila. There is a memorial window in the west end of the church to another daughter of his who died on her 33rd birthday. Savage also took the photographs that were used to illustrate Humbert's *History*—the first use of that medium in a substantial local history.

Humbert was perhaps fortunate that one of the residents, Brother King, had been a mason. Although almost eighty, he had fixed up his own scaffolding, and did much work in cleaning the walls of the church. Indeed, alone he scoured the two chapels. Later, he was joined by the Hon. Alan Brodrick, and, with him, was partly responsible for cleaning and repairing a great deal of the plaster work in the church. Brother King is remembered in a simple stone in the Peace Chapel with the inscription 'James King, Brother of this Hospital. Died April 12th., 1877, aged 91. Formerly a mason of this city'.

Some heating was introduced, although the architect commented: 'I do not propose to heat the church so much with a view to the comfort of the congregation as to making it dry and healthy'. Modern congregations sometimes still feel that that objective alone has been achieved. The font, which was in the north aisle by Peter de Sancta Maria's tomb, was moved to the south-west corner 'as it interferes with the convenient arrangement of a congregation'. The screens crossing from north to south in the east end were removed, and seating was placed for the brethren on the north and south sides of the choir, below the tower, with a bench at the front for the 'singing men'.

In accordance with Butterfield's first assessment in 1858, the floor was relaid on brick piers, and so raised from the earth, providing the drying effect he sought. Encaustic tiles were laid down. New doors were made, following the original pattern. By this time, all the money that was available for building repairs had been spent, and it seemed that the work must stop.

At this stage, what must have seemed like a miracle occurred. On 11 August 1863, a letter, signed simply Z.O., post marked Cowes, arrived. It contained a cheque for £500, which was to be used to restore the church around the communion table, and to replace the four plain glass windows over that table with stained glass. The donor wished that the initials of the Queen, Prince Consort, Bishop and Master should be incorporated. The old tiles in the church could also be relaid in front of the communion table. Butterfield suggested that there would be too much wear on tiles by the communion table, and Z.O. wrote agreeing, but asked that the stained glass be provided by Wailes of Newcastle, who had provided other glass in the church. The Trustees gratefully accepted the money and all the suggestions. Two sets of the central windows at the east end proudly show VR and

AP for Victoria and Albert. To the north, the window holds the initials CW, being those of the archdeacon rather than the Bishop. Humbert is LMH in the south window, although a quick look would suggest a W rather than an H. In front of the altar rail, Z.O. is commemorated, his initials being incorporated into the tiles.

Butterfield pressed ahead with the work, being urged by impatient Trustees in January 1864 to make haste still further. Once more it seemed that the money was going to run out, and once more Z.O. came to the rescue, this time with a donation of £250. Of course, everyone was curious about Z.O.'s identity. Rev. Humbert wrote and asked for further names so that he could write direct, rather than via the G.P.O. in London. Besides, the Post Office said that they made it a rule never to deliver letters addressed by initials only. There was no response. Slight clues existed. Z.O. had said that he had once visited St Cross on his travels and been much impressed with its beauty. Linguists could twist Z.O. to mean Zum Osborne—to Osborne. Recently, on a journey to Osborne, the Prince of Wales had visited St Cross. He spoke English with a German accent. Both of the Prince's parents were to be remembered in the windows. Despite its rules, the Post Office continued to deliver letters addressed by initials only. Clearly, Z.O. was a man of some influence. Therefore, St Cross maintains, the mystery donor was Edward, Prince of Wales. There is no proof one way or the other, and the mystery remains unsolved to this day.

Lack of a functioning organ was a considerable handicap in a church which loved music. Humbert arranged with Walker's to build and erect a new instrument. The money was raised by yet more activities throughout the parish, arranged by the indefatigable Master, during the winter of 1862 and the early part of 1863, when the work was completed.

Naturally, what was provided for the brethren was of key importance to the Trustees. When they looked at the various allowances which were made 'one matter which at once attracted the attention of the Committee was the extraordinary amount of beer (3 quarts) which each Brother receives daily—a quantity which is evidently much more than they can require'. There were also extras at various times so that the total 'is much greater than the Brethren can possibly consume'. Consequently, the ration was reduced to two quarts per day. All upright Victorians looked on 'The Demon Drink' with horror, so this reduction would seem both morally correct and economically convenient. The brethren refused the offer of money in place of the food allowances. They were now given 22oz. of bread every day, instead of on five days only. Ordinary commons were continued throughout Lent instead of a money allowance and an annual allowance of one and a half tons of coal was made. Regular meals of meat were provided and it was estimated that the cost to the Trustees per brother would be about £1 per week. There were to be six special days— All Saints' Eve, Christmas Eve, Easter Eve, Invention of the Cross, Whitsun Eve, Founder's Day, when extra food and drink would be provided. The daily Wayfarers' Dole would be continued, but in the form of 32 quarter pints of beer and two 22 oz. loaves of bread sliced into 22 portions. There was no explanation why there should be 10 extra quarter pints of beer, as compared with the bread issued. The custom of issuing bread at the gates, or a half-penny in lieu, on the six special days, was ended, as the committee felt that the weak and deserving poor got pushed out by the strong and perhaps undeserving. Thus the last remnants of the Hundred Menne's Hall poor charity came to be those people on pensions as provided for in the scheme from 1858.

The special position of Brother Stubbington was carefully considered. He was the Porter, distributed the Wayfarers' Dole and was supposed to keep the grounds clean and tidy. He also earned about £45 per year as 'Exhibitor', or guide, getting tips from the visitors he showed round the Hospital. It was felt that he was too old and infirm to continue his duties as Porter, but that he could remain as exhibitor. However, in future visitors would be expected to buy an entry ticket, varying from 6d. for one to 1s. 6d for more than three. Stubbington would be entitled to one-third of the proceeds, a third would go to the burial fund for brethren, and the remaining third towards providing a reading room for those who lived in.

The reading room became fact shortly, and a list of books provided suggests that modern brothers would not be too happy with the choice. There was *The Life of Lord Chancellor Hardcastle* (3 vols.), *The lives of the Lord Chancellors* (3 vols.) *History of the Tower*, *North West Passage by Land*, *Arctic Land Expedition*, *Constantinople during the Crimean War*, *Polish Captivity*, *African Hunting from Natal to the Zambezi*, and a number more in the same vein. True, Victorian reading was rather more serious than present day, but one has difficulty in thinking of these books as being much read, improving though they may have been.

There were a number of empty rooms. Humbert and the Trustees decided to start a rolling repair scheme, putting empty rooms into good condition, until eventually all the rooms would have been repaired. Brother Stubbington's room was panelled, as paper would not stick to the damp walls! The main push was to ensure that all brethren's rooms were properly painted, that water was laid on to all rooms, that each brother had efficient washing facilities, and that their toilets were effective and hygienic. For their part, the brothers complained that the beer was too weak, and that the meat was not up to standard. The Trustees met a deputation to discuss the matter and, in the event, changed the supplier in each case. 'The Trustees would not consider trifling any matter which may affect the comfort of the brethren.'

Sub-committees of the Trustees were set up, and one, the Visiting Committee, was given the task of keeping in close touch with the brothers. Sometimes, they had to take unpleasant action. Brother Wilkins, who was deaf and almost eighty, was warned in 1860 about his 'wanton behaviour' with certain women in the wooded area beyond the Hospital walls. Apparently, he persisted. There is a beautifully copper-plated description of the second time he was brought before the Committee. He could scarcely hear what was said, so it all had to be written down clearly for him. He was accused of 'immoral behaviour' with women of the area in the waste ground, and was deprived of his gown and badge, and dismissed from the Hospital. One does not know whether to condemn his stupidity in continuing with the same line of action, or to admire his ability at his age to do twice something that earned a warning. Perhaps his deafness meant that he was also unable to hear anyone say 'no'! Another brother, Brother Hayward, was warned not to work in his son's shop, and told not to go out without his gown on.

One recurring feature in the accounts of 1859, '60, and '61 was £2 2s. 0d. for the rat-catcher. As work was done around the Hospital and as the gardens behind the brothers' quarters were brought back into use, so the area of rats' nests was disturbed. It was essential to keep the numbers down if the health of the brethren were not to suffer. Hence the rat-catcher. Providing for the brethren's comfort in another way, the barber was told to shave the brothers twice a week instead of just once as had been done hitherto.

As the houses were repaired, so there was room for new brothers. Five were installed in October 1857—Brothers George Maton, John Griffiths, Joseph Coffe, Thomas Henry Hayward, Jacob Keeling. From this date onwards, the numbers on the Hospital foundation of de Blois were kept at a reasonable level.

Like his great predecessor, de Campeden, Humbert must have been a most effective fund raiser, for a great deal of work was done that was not paid for out of the closely controlled funds of the Charity. There were too many bills, such as about £6,000 to pay for the Chancery case, to allow for free expenditure. On one occasion, not entirely to his surprise, he was unsuccessful. He wrote to Lord Guilford, suggesting that he might perhaps like to present a chalice to the church as a memorial to the pleasant days he had spent at St Cross. Guilford wrote back: 'Deprived of my rights as I have been by the Court of Chancery, I am perhaps the very last person to whom application should be made for a

39   *The scene in the Brethren's Hall after the reopening of the church in 1865. Note the Prince of Wales' feathers on the wall at the far end, above the Master, in deference to the belief that Z. O. was the Prince of Wales.*

donation to the Hospital. The heavy debt you mention would not exist had not the Master of the Rolls forced me from my office, and deprived the Corporation of its chartered property, and placed it in other hands. To those hands I must refer you.'

In an attempt to draw attention to the Hospital buildings, and to weld together the whole group of people living within its walls, the master gave occasional dinners in the Brethren's Hall. For almost twelve months, from the end of 1864, the church had to be closed because of the amount of restoration work taking place. At length, in 1865, it was thought that enough work had been done to justify rededicating the church. The Bishop of Winchester preached the sermon, and, as the local and national press noted, a goodly company of influential people attended a dinner in the Hall. Certainly, as a public relation exercise, the whole day was a success, and led to another £500 being immediately added to the funds, with promises which were at length to total a further £2,500.

Humbert is credited with at least reviving a custom which, by its nature, is unique to St Cross. When a brother dies, one of the gates leading into the Beaufort Tower is closed, and the other left open. The symbolism behind this is to show that while a gate of earthly life has closed, the gate to eternal life has, at the same time, opened.

When Humbert died, he was buried in the cemetery to the south west of the church. He certainly ranks as one of the great Masters, for his was the motive force behind all the work that was done immediately after the Chancery case. The present Hospital owes him much for the solid foundations he built. Just inside the church—indeed, almost the first stone on which worshippers tread as they pass through the inner doors—is a memorial to him and one to his wife. It is fitting that his stone and that of de Campeden should lie where present-day worshippers can hardly avoid being in touch with these great past Masters, who did so much to ensure that the Hospital continued to exist in difficult times.

CHAPTER *XIII*

Into the Twentieth Century

George Lewing, one of the brothers who lived in St Cross under Humbert's successor, Rev. Andrewes, kept a diary from 1873 to 1896. George had been a schoolmaster at Sunningdale and then Headmaster of St John the Baptist School at Aston Cantaloe. When he decided to apply to St Cross, he organised the whole affair with great efficiency. Apart from filling in the usual form, he visited the Warden of Winchester College, who told him that he was too young for the Charity. Next, he called on the Dean of the Cathedral, who explained that there was no present vacancy, but that he would bear him in mind if one occurred. Finally, he called on 'Mr. Barrow-Simonds, M.P., at his home'. Barrow Simonds had been a Trustee almost from the very start, and he was to give many years good and important service both as Trustee and as Chairman. In the north transept, there are a number of memorial windows to his family. He said that Lewing was 'too young: upwards of one hundred and twenty candidates, but no vacancy. I ought to present myself to the Master.' Lewing had to return to Aston Cantaloe before seeing the Master, but his visits bore fruit, as four months later he was elected as a brother of the Hospital foundation.

In time, he held office as sexton and, later, librarian. As sexton, he was interested in death. He recorded at various times the suicides of Brothers Robinson, Lindon and Groundsele. One had hanged himself from a tree in the garden ('the third from the pond'), a second had hanged himself out of his front window, and the third had committed suicide in his closet. Brother J. Southcott was the first to be buried in the new gowns. Brother James Bligh Scott was recorded as 'a very worthy, kind hearted brother'. Indeed, many of his final comments on brothers are praising the dead.

When Brother Finch died, his badge, by mistake, was buried with him, and left Brother Leach, his successor, without a badge until the grave could be reopened. Lewing thereupon wrote a detailed description of what happened after a brother's death, in the hopes that such a mistake might not again occur. The dead man's coffin was taken into the Hall and placed on trestles in the centre. The rest of the brothers then came in, sat round about the catafalque, and silently ate a slice of bread and drank a pint of beer. The deceased's relatives were expected to provide a bottle of gin and a cake for the brethren to share after the interment. Before the coffin was taken out, the silver badge of the Charity was taken from the dead man's gown, ready to be passed on to the next brother to be appointed. The bearers at the funeral were rewarded with a jack of beer. The procession to the graveside was headed by the Porter, bearing a veiled staff. Rev. Andrewes introduced a brothers' meeting, where matters of daily routine were discussed. The system of beer, gin and cake at funerals was ended by a vote of this group in October 1881.

A later Master, Rev. Charles Bostock, discovered that the staff carried at funerals itself had a somewhat odd history. He thought that it was a veiled processional cross. Taking off the veiling, he discovered that it was in fact cardboard covered at the top. Talking with Rev. Andrewes' son (himself a canon), he was told that, when the church was re-opened in 1865, it was thought that a suitable staff should be carried before the Bishop. When Butterfield was approached, he said he would provide one. This he did by cutting off a poppy-head from an old pew and mounting it on a staff. The poppy-head would seem to be of the 16th-century style. This has led to an attribution as Bishop Fox's pastoral staff, used when he visited St Cross. Canon Andrewes could remember seeing the pew from which the poppy head had been cut. After the reopening of the church, the top of the staff was surrounded in cardboard to give an easier shape for winding crepe around, and it was then carried in funeral processions. As the staff had such a poor pedigree, Bostock gave orders for the custom to cease in 1939.

Drink remained a source of trouble through to the 1930s. In Andrewes' time as Master, David Shield was expelled for drunken behaviour, although Lewing sums him up as 'A man clever as an artist and of a kind disposition'. Warned, but not expelled, was Brother Stretton. He had been 'caught intoxicated by the Master, and seen by others several times in Winchester, St Cross'. He was told that he would be dismissed if he repeated the behaviour. Thomas Bowsher, the Porter, was found in 1899 to have been 'recently intoxicated ... and was prohibited from entering any public house in Saint Cross'. Presumably, it was safe to go into the Winchester ones! Thereafter, it became the custom to warn a brother on first offence and dismiss him for a repetition.

The first Trustees had reduced the daily beer ration. In one of the brothers' meetings, the question of the allowance was raised. Most of those present felt that it was not an advantage to have it, and all agreed that it would be much better if a money equivalent were to replace it. Consequently, on 9 January 1877, Lewing records in his diary, 'The last allowance of beer from the malt. In future, will receive 3s 0d per week instead'.

Lewing was greatly intrigued by the case of Richard Cheyne, who had been a brother in Lord Guilford's time. Whilst at the Hospital, he had become very friendly with a family called Woolgar in Otterbourne. He frequently was allowed away from St Cross to spend time with his new friends. Woolgar had property from which he collected rents. One collection day, he was found murdered at his house, with all the rent money missing. Cheyne was suspected, and his rooms at the Hospital carefully searched, but nothing was found. Woolgar's son continued the friendship with Cheyne, but also contacted 'the Bow Street Runner, Lavender', who was looking for a William Parsons, reputed to be mad, and a multi-murderer from Ratcliffe. One day, when young Woolgar was alone in the house, Cheyne came in and attacked him. Fortunately, Lavender was hot on the trail, rushed in, and arrested Cheyne, identifying him as Parsons. Lewing copied the story from the summer edition of St James' magazine.

In digging a grave, George came across an older, minor graveyard. He uncovered 20 skeletons, of which only four were in wooden coffins, the rest being in rough chalk casings. He kept a piece of chalk of which he wrote:

This piece of chalk once formed a portion of the covering of a chalk grave in which reposed a skeleton, apparently of a young woman, probably co-eval with the building of St Cross Hospital. In her grave was found some worked chalk forming the crown of an arch or doorway at a depth of 5 feet or thereabouts, and some large flint, and in the N.E. angle of the grave, a portion of work as if the church were part of a walling. Part of a roofing tile was also found very slightly burned.

The graves were clearly of a date before the present St Cross, and may have had some connection with the buildings it replaced. The burned tiles do tie in with the story of a Viking destruction of an earlier church or monastery. If, however, it had been a monastery, the presence of a skeleton of a young woman there is a mystery.

The phrase 'once in a blue moon' was disproved by Brother Lewing. On 5 November 1883, he wrote, '4 p.m. Saw the moon distinctly of a steel or silver blue colour'. Next day, he again wrote, 'Early moon still to be observed as of a blue colour gradually fading with the setting sun'.

Food was a preoccupation of the brothers and Lewing often wrote about it in his diary. 'The pork ordered for this day's dinner of the brethren said to be scarcely eatable and by some not able to eat it at all, and those who had mutton said gravy tainted with Pork dripping rendered their dinner very nauseous, but the matter certain of the brethren wished to keep quiet.' 'The leg of mutton supplied for this day looking not very pleasant to the eye, having cut up the neck and divided into 3 portions according to our usual practice. On proceeding to do so in like manner with the Leg, I was forbidden to do so by the Brethren present until it had been shown to the Revd. the Master by the Brothers present. The Master having been summoned saw the said leg, ordered me to cut a piece out, which having been done, he, after due examination, etc., by Self, etc, declared the same to be good. The Brethren leaving the same and the stock with the cook, the Master declared it forfeited.' Dripping was regarded very highly, and the brothers were carefully regulated in the amount each received, largely according to seniority. Similarly, seniority was important in collecting walnuts from the park for pickling. The Senior Brother was allowed to pick from 'the first tree in the south park and the furthest one outside the court, towards Winchester'. On one occasion, George records that his share was 'about 220' nuts. All took part in the ceremony of whipping the walnut trees, which was believed to improve the yield. The old practice of topping and lopping still persisted and, when he was Senior Brother, Lewing insisted to the Trustees that the right should be continued. Taking into account rations and cash payments, but not including anything else (flat, heating, clothes, etc.), Lewing estimated that a brother received support to the annual value of £39 15s. 5d. This would have represented a quite considerable salary by itself, but was, of course, much increased by the receipt of free housing, clothes and heating. The brethren of the late 19th century were comparatively well off as a result.

The Trustees were also interested in questions of meat and drink. 'As three of the Gaudy Days occur within one fortnight, it would be desirable to change two of them to some other days, and they accordingly suggest Easter Monday and Whitsun Monday.' The extraordinary commons on special days are 'much greater than the Brethren can possibly consume' and were reduced. One special item was provided on Good Friday. It was called 'Judas Sop' and consisted of bread boiled in beer, honey and spices.

Light was slowly brought into the area. Gas lighting was put into the quad in 1870, and, next year, into the long passages and rooms of the Master's lodge. At this stage, the brothers were still walking around with candles. To help them to find their way to their own quarters, their rooms were given numbers for the first time. Electric light came to the Master's house, Chaplain's quarters and the brethren's flats in 1901. To conserve power, the Master controlled a central switch and turned off all electricity at 10.00p.m. when everyone returned to reliance on candles. Not until 1928 was the system changed and the electricity left available all night, 'because of the danger of old men carrying candles'. Another modern amenity, taken for granted now, was the introduction of mains sewerage in 1879, when 'the pits' in St Cross were joined up to the main drain by excavations stretching from 'the Avenue, from The Bell to Frog Lane' (now Back Lane).

The diary records also the human side of George's family life. In 1873, he wrote 'Edith Lewing, my grandchild came to bide with me'. There are records of other visits, such as from son Charles and grand-daughter Alice, but Edith was obviously more locally based and perhaps a favourite, as she was most often mentioned. Eventually, Lewing says, 'Edith went as indoor servant to Mrs. Knight, 65, Kingsgate at 4s. 4d. per year, to be allowed to come and see me once a week, to go to church every Sunday'. Even allowing for the fact that the post was one in which all was found, 4s. 4d. does strike a cold note for a year's salary, and compares badly with what Lewing estimated he himself received.

When the railways came to Winchester, St Cross had to surrender some land for the line through 'St Faith's Parish'. Obviously, the carriages were not heated, as Lewing mentions that, 'At noon, booked a shawl for Mrs. Turner at the railway station'. Another form of transport he noted was the balloon. On one day in 1874, he saw 'the balloon and the flying man'. Next day, he records soberly that the balloon had crashed and the flying man been killed. In the same year, he noted a comet passing through the skies.

A number of military gentlemen and priests became inmates under Andrewes. Lewing records that the brethren objected to them using their titles. Once they came into St Cross, they were Brothers, and nothing else. It was pointed out that a man who became Reverend remained so all his life, unless unfrocked. Nevertheless, the Brethren voted overwhelmingly that the only title which might be used should be 'Brother'.

Reformation of the electoral system was something that took up much parliamentary time in the 1880s. There were two reform bills, in 1884 and 1885, but the franchise remained far from universal for men, and still excluded women. Brother Lewing noted in 1888 'Revd. the Master expressed his displeasure at several brothers having their names placed on the voters register without first obtaining permission from him'. It is incredible that a man who looked after his charges as conscientiously and kindly as did Rev. Andrewes should apparently feel that he had the right to deny them the vote to which they might be entitled.

There are a number of references to dinners and teas which the Master provided for the brethren. In 1880, for instance, Lewing records with apparent pleasure that 'The Master gave the Brothers tea in his house and a lecture on Egypt and Palestine with reference to the journeyings of the Children of Israel with scenic illustrations'. It was certainly a different vision of entertainment from that held today!

Amongst the special occasions was the marriage of the Master's son. There was a choral service at St Cross, led by a joint choir of 40 men and boys from Highcliffe and St Cross. In triumph, Lewing notes 'Fifteen carriages!', 'St. Faith's women (70) tea'd in the hall. School children (84) at Bell Inn and sports in field opposite. The Master gave each brother a bottle of port.' Interesting to find the women in the Hall, but the children in the pub! He also records a swift courtship in 1876. 'Hester Prior, aged 49, daughter of the late Brother Prior, married to Mr. G. Coward, widower for the 3rd. time and having an independency. Aged 67, in St Cross Church, by Licence, 9 a.m. Son of the said G.C acting as father and his daughter as Ladies Bridesmaid. Commenced his suit to her Monday, 11th. Inst., received her final reply on the 13th.,took out licence for 18th., ordered van for removal of her goods same day. She removed from St. Cross on the 20th. The whole affair courtship and matrimony occupying 10 days.'

Lewing also saw the return of one of the great treasures of the Cathedral to its proper place. '19 and 20 April, 1888. After 22 years, the chandeliers taken back to the Cathedral again.' These were the two large chandeliers given to the Dean and Chapter by Dean Cheyney over one hundred years previously, which had come to St Cross at its reopening.

National events sometimes touched the quiet community. There were many wars in this period of Victorian imperialism and, as a garrison town, Winchester saw its fair share of soldiers coming and going. '26th. March, 1874. 2nd. Rifle Brigade returned from war in Ashanti. Flag hoisted, St Cross. No beer given extra, as had been done heretofore, for which I am very glad indeed.'

When the Order of Noble Poverty was brought back to life in 1881, there were 10 applicants for only two places at the time. The first elected was Henry Thomas Stephen who had sent in a printed application for the Hospital foundation as far back as 1873. He had been a book-keeper in the coach station at Southampton, and later an inn-keeper. He was 68 and the log states laconically, about his health 'Not bad considering age'. John Twigge was the second man elected. He had been 'a schoolmaster and usher. In 1875, the School in which he was Usher was taken over by the National Schools and he was unable through failing sight to obtain the necessary Government Certificate.' He was 71. This was the period following the great Education Act of 1870, when religious bodies and the state squabbled over the provision of education. Where state schools developed, religious bodies soon found that their buildings or staff did not measure up to certain criteria. Twigge held testimonials from five priests, and it can be seen that he was a victim of the church failing to hold on to its school in his area. He was not alone in this fate.

Towards the end of Rev. Andrewes' period of office, rumblings of discontent began to show themselves in the Trustees' minute book. Brother Dicker complained that his wife had been upset by foul language used by Brother Rogers' wife whilst she was intoxicated. Rogers agreed that the offence had occurred as his wife 'was given to drink'. However, she had now taken the pledge and it was hoped all would be well. He was warned that repetition would mean expulsion from St Cross. Presumably, the pledge was effective, as the two Rogers remained living in the Hospital.

Food continued to be an important item. 'Certain discontent among some of the Brethren with regard to their food allowances' is reported. Bread supplied by Dumper was claimed by the brethren to be sub-standard. The Trustees investigated all complaints, decided that there was nothing wrong, but wished to free themselves from further trouble. In future a weekly allowance of 8s. 9d. would be made to replace the rations.

Despite any internal difficulties, St Cross still emanated a sense of calm. Walter Dendy Sadler, R.A., walked through the park, and was impressed by the monastic appearance of St Cross. He used it as the back-drop for his painting *Thursday* (sometimes mis-named *Tomorrow will be Friday*), showing monks fishing in the Itchen.

By 1896, the Trustees had decided that it would be a good idea to convert the Master's house, now forming most of the northern side of the quad, into brethren's accommodation. The Master was in favour of the idea, but looked for a new house for himself to be built to the east of Beaufort's Tower, and in the garden. At first, the Trustees agreed. Then, the architect, Sir Arthur Blomfield, having produced a plan for this area, was asked to consider the orchard, outside the walls of St Cross, as a suitable place for the new home. Another plan was produced, which the Trustees accepted. Andrewes was totally against it, feeling that the site would be too damp, and the house was too small—he needed at least four reception rooms. The five bedrooms were too small, ranging in width from 8 feet to 11 feet. In a minute of July 1896 he said 'The plans which I have seen fall very far short of what I expected, and therefore I decline to give up my house and garden or to move any further in the matter'. The Trustees could not agree with him, so he wrote a letter of complaint to the Charity Commissioners, which was rejected. Eventually, the new house was built in 1899, but Andrewes simply refused to go and live in it. He was, by now, in failing health, and the Trustees agreed to allow him to continue in the old site (they really had no other option), and let off the new house to the Chaplain. For a large part of the second half of 1900, the Master was unable to carry out his duties. Indeed, the Visiting Committee effected much of the liaison between the charities and the beneficiaries. Andrewes had been a good and caring Master, but in February 1901 he resigned his office, as he was no longer able to do the job properly. Just before this, the Trustees had voted an extra £150 per year to him, dependent on 'the due performance of his duties'. When a new scheme was produced by the Charity Commissioners in 1901, it included a specific clause permitting Andrewes to go on living in his current house, even though he had resigned and a new Master had been appointed. He remained there until his death in 1903. Nine years later, the whole set of rooms was converted into more accommodation for brothers, a library-cum-billiard room, a Master's Office, and a board room for the Trustees.

The new man was Canon the Hon. Alan Brodrick, who had already spent some time helping to clean the walls, under Butterfield. He was aware at his appointment that the Trustees, because of their respect for Andrewes, and their recognition of his poor state of health, allowed his predecessor to live in what was now his freehold. There was also left hanging in the air the possibility of some ill-feeling because of the award of £150 as long as Andrewes carried out his duties properly, at least hinting that the Trustees felt he had not done so. It cannot have been an easy situation within which to work. He moved into the new Master's house, thus, in a sense, returning to the earliest days of St Cross. Once more, the Master lived away from the brethren and to the north of them, outside the walls of the Hospital. He was also strangely isolated from the Master's garden, which still lies to the east of the Porter's lodge, formerly the Master's lodge.

40   *The Master's lodge and Chaplain's lodge, originally built in 1900 as the Master's house.*

There was some continuity in the Trustees. When Brodrick was appointed, they were, apart from those *ex officio*, Lord Northbrook, Lord Selborne (who resigned shortly on his appointment as Minister of War, whilst the Boer War was ending), Lord Montagu of Beaulieu, W. Barrow Simonds, M.G. Knight, J. Lindsay Johnson, J.C. Moberly, Sir W. Spencer Portal, Col. Heathcote and W.G. Nicholson, M.P. The Duke of Wellington was elected shortly after.

At the start of the 20th century, St Cross still owned enough properties to be involved in regular expenses as landlords. A grant of £25 was made to Litton towards the re-hanging of its bells. Twyford received £10 for heating the chancel. A similar work at Yately led to a £14 gift. Colden Common received £25 for its parish hall and club, plus £50 for the school. Aldershot's chancel was repaired. St Faith's burial ground attracted £245, with a further £50 to the school. Long Selborne and Whitchurch were each granted £250 for their schools. Special grants were made to the Cove Coal and Clothing Club, the local charities at Crondal and the Farnborough poor. Fareham's chancel was repaired by the Trustees. £125 was given to provide a vestry and organ at St Mary Bourne. Grants of this type were repeatedly made throughout the various parishes over the years.

There were, in addition to lands and houses in each of the parishes mentioned above (especially Litton), many properties in and around Winchester, Longparish, Fordingbridge,

Ellingham, and Ashton. There were still some almost medieval rents. For instance, both the Earl of Portsmouth in Hurstbourne and St Mary Bourne, and Captain Frost in Owslebury, were supposed to pay in wheat and malt. In fact, of course, they paid cash based on the market value of the produce they were expected to render. Not until 1926, with the death of Mrs. Falwasser, did the last of the renting by lives end. This event alone brought in extra income of £445 per annum from the tithes of Owslebury.

There were domestic difficulties. Sir Arthur Blomfield, the architect, in February 1901, observed: 'I think that steps should be taken to stop the practice of throwing refuse water, etc., out of the scullery windows. The state of the walls under those windows, in addition to the bed of the water-way, is sufficient evidence of the frequency of this practice; even when I was examining the buildings a basin of garbage of some description was thrown out of one of the upper windows.' The same report suggests that electric light be laid on to the Master's house, and that there should be 'water upstairs in the bath room so that servants can draw hot water without descending to the ground floor'.

On occasions, Trustees came into the grounds and gave instructions for minor repairs to be done on the spot. Blomfield felt that this procedure was demeaning to him and complained. He was rebuffed and told to make his monthly inspections more detailed, as this would have removed the need for Trustees to act. There were further passages of arms when some of the windows in the Master's house let in water. Blomfield was told plainly that he should never have passed the building and the responsibility for repair rested on him. When he presented a bill for £118 0s. 7d. for other work, the Trustees refused to pay. In due course, the error was put right, and the bill was paid.

During 1906, Mrs. Brodrick died. She had played a full part in the life of the Hospital and parish. To commemorate her, the Master installed a 30-hour clock in the tower and repaired and completed the organ. Parishioners felt her loss also, and refurbished and refurnished the south chapel in her memory. The Trustees took advantage of this work to move the triptych from its place in the Hall and hang it over the altar in the chapel.

The new organ was a splendid instrument and Brodrick reported that he felt the organist, Mr. Gamblin, to be too old to do it justice. The Trustees minuted that the Master should 'intimate that his past services could be recognised in some way if he desired to retire.' Mr. Gamblin decided that he did so desire and received a pension of £30 a year. Two years later, the organ was given electric power, and the organ blower also retired on a pension of £10 per year.

The Brodricks were no doubt a family of above average wealth, but equally they found occasion to spend that wealth for the benefit of St Cross. When his son died, Canon Brodrick gave the money for the Church Hall in Back Lane, whose use benefited the parishioners rather more than the brethren.

An Act of 1908 led to considerable discussion amongst the Trustees. Parliament had introduced a non-contributory Old Age Pension, due to be paid for the first time on 1 January to anyone over 70. It was to be 5s. per week, but only 7s. 6d. for a married couple living together. Anyone with an income of 10s. a week or more was debarred from receiving the pension. Many of those in St Cross, on either foundation, would be affected. This raised the question of state benefits *vis-à-vis* Hospital payments. It was decided that all the men in the Hospital should register for state benefits, and it was resolved to reduce

Hospital pensions to 5s. per week where brethren were likely to be eligible for a state pension.

In 1908, Canon Brodrick asked to be allowed to replace the roodbeam and cross in their old place in the church. The Trustees agreed and plans were drawn up. Before they could be put into action, Canon Brodrick died suddenly in the spring of 1909. However, the beam and cross were replaced as a visible memorial to the Master. His period of office was immensely valuable in laying down further firm foundations upon which to build. Both parish and Hospital benefited from his work.

CHAPTER XIV

Towards 2000

Canon Causton took St Cross through the pre-war period, the First World War and post-war years. He was faced almost immediately with the problem of the position of St Faith's. There was clearly a physical parish of St Faith, but there was no church attached. The query was whether the parishioners were entitled to elect churchwardens to a non-existent church. The answer was that the election could take place, as a civil parish existed, but those elected could claim no jurisdiction within St Cross. This was further confirmed at a later date, but churchwardens are allowed to act within St Cross, whose church is the centre of worship for the parish of St Faith. Legally, the church and Hospital buildings remain extra-parochial, and so do not form part of a parish. Whereas formerly, the brethren carried out all the duties (sidesman, bell-ringer etc.) within the church, now, in 1994, they are shared between parishioners of St Faith and the brothers of St Cross.

Up to Causton's time, brethren had worn hats of their own choice. Often this meant bowler, billy-cock, or top hats. In 1913, the Trustees decided to arrange for all brethren to wear soft hats, very much in the style of those worn in Tudor times. For the Hospital Foundation they were black, whilst the Noble Poverty wore red. It was felt that this would add to the dignity of the charities. Another matter which apparently affected dignity was the ownership of 32-38 Upper Brook Street. These properties were sold 'owing to the character of the neighbourhood and the difficulty there is in obtaining suitable tenants'.

For some reason, in 1912, the architect, Sir. T.G. Jackson, had the calvary on the south wall whitewashed over. By custom, he had not attended Trustees' meetings, but sent a written report. None of the members knew why this action had been taken, and he was asked to explain it. His next quarterly written report had no explanation, so he was once more asked the same question. This went on at each quarterly meeting to 1914, when other issues took priority. Part of this calvary, some twenty feet by twelve feet in size, has been uncovered in a preliminary examination in 1994.

Even peaceful St Cross could not entirely ignore domestic politics. From July 1912, Christabel Pankhurst orchestrated an increasingly violent series of attacks on property, in support of the votes for women campaign. As empty and occupied houses were set on fire, the Trustees felt that they should protect the buildings of St Cross and employed a night watchman, due 'to the risk of attacks by militant suffragettes on ancient buildings'.

Soon, such violence was swallowed up in the greater violence of the First World War. Sadly, the Trustees note that ticket sales had fallen, a result they blamed on the war. In

41   *Edwardian brothers of the Hospital Foundation, showing the variety of headgear worn.*

1915, the War Office took over 'stables, cow pens and yard lying between the Brethren's gardens and the main road to accommodate their horses. The same remark applies to the Master's stables.' Later, war regulations led to the Trustees becoming involved with one of their tenants. The War Agricultural Committee told Mr. Waters, a tenant at Whitchurch, that his land was in a bad state and that his husbandry was not up to standard. The Trustees made inquiries to find out why this was so and what had to be done. Mr. Waters explained that his horse had had the mange, but was better, and that he would be able to do all the necessary work now.

A year later, Mr. Way, the Receiver, asked the Trustees to support his claim for exemption from military call-up, because of the important work for them in which he was involved. However, the Trustees refused to do so, in view 'of the present grave emergency'. This was the time of Ludendorff's great offensive on the Somme, when Haig was appealing desperately for every man he could lay hands on and begging the Americans to start fighting, even if they were as yet scarcely organised. Haig was successful, the war ended, and Way stayed at home.

Bearing in mind his ancestry, it was no surprise to find the Duke of Wellington suggesting to his fellow Trustees that they should change the terms of their constitution to enable them to give financial or other aid to disabled soldiers and sailors, regardless of age or income—an echo of what Lisle had done under the Protectorate. The Charity Commissioners, however, would not permit any variation, though such men could be enrolled under the normal conditions.

As early as January, 1917, the Master suggested that the North Chapel should become a memorial chapel to the fallen. This was a particularly poignant suggestion, coming from him, as he lost a son in action in 1918. It was decided to commission Sir George Frampton to produce a bronze statuette of St George. Mrs. Morris gave the east window entitled 'Fortitude', and it was agreed to provide a Portland stone altar, and oak rails. On 14 October 1918, the Peace Chapel was dedicated, listing the war dead of St Cross. It must surely be the earliest chapel of its kind, since the war did not end until November.

The war had its lesser effects on the Hospital. In December 1917 it was found impossible to hold the Christmas Gaudy as there was a shortage of meat. Instead, the brothers all received a special allowance of 3s. 6d.

After the war, the depression and bad weather combined to affect the income available. Many of the rent and tithe payers were from agricultural areas. The Receiver reported 'that St Mary Bourne Parish, where arrears are heaviest, is a poor agricultural district, and the unfavourable weather during the past year has prejudiced the tithe payers'. It was not until the Second World War that many of the arrears were cleared. Trustees felt that, as a charity, they could not be too harsh on those suffering through no fault of their own. Yet, equally, they had to press for payment so that their own charity did not suffer.

When the General Strike occurred, in 1926, and was continued for a further six months by the miners alone, the Hospital could not obtain coal in sufficient quantity for its needs. The only way to heat the rooms was to get doctors' notes for the brethren, so that each could obtain an independent fuel supply. Thus, instead of receiving the actual coal, the men were given a cash payment. This could not have been a great source of warmth and comfort to those old men who were unable to obtain medical support.

In 1926, Causton inaugurated the first attempts to remove Butterfield's wall colouring—referred to in the minutes as the 'unfortunate stencilling on the walls'. Bit by bit, the walls were returned to a more acceptable, in modern eyes, plain stone colour. Soon after this, in the autumn of 1927, Causton retired and, as a very special favour, was allowed to take his Master's badge with him. This alone would be sufficient to show the high regard in which he was held by the Trustees. It was stated that this was not to be regarded as a pattern for the future, although the families of the next two Masters did, in fact, take the badges with them on leaving St Cross.

His successor was the Archdeacon of Winchester, the Ven. Daldy. He at once had the original altar stone of de Campeden moved from the base of the altar to form its top. One other alteration within the church was carried out. In 1929, the vestry was divided into two halves, by putting up an oak screen, leaving one side for the choir and the other for the clergy.

In the same year there were questions about the money coming into the Charity. There must have been murmurs of fear that peculation had crept in again. The regular auditing showed that a sum of £365 18s. 6d. had been paid to the Hospital, but did not appear in any cash book. Further investigations showed yet other irregularities over cash receipts, books not kept up to date, and bankings not done. Philip S. Way, the Receiver, who had held office since 1917, resigned, and was succeeded by Alan Arnold. Until then it had been the duty of the Receiver to interview all candidates for either pensions or entry as inmates. Now it was decided that the Master should interview those who wished to live in, but that the Receiver should see the out-pensioners. To make things financially safer if failings should occur in book-keeping, the Trustees took out a fidelity insurance policy on the Receiver.

Occasionally, people referred to the church as a chapel. Trustees wished to discover its real designation. In April 1928, they received a letter from Mrs. Eleanor Cottrill, the County Archivist and Diocesan Records Officer, saying that St Cross had been designated a church since at least 1298, and should be so described. Later, the word 'chapel' crept in again, and the archivist asked that it be once more minuted that the name was 'Church'. So in 1994, the true designation was confirmed.

An internal change of title was made in 1933. Previously, the assistant clergyman had always been called the curate. Often, however, he was an experienced clergyman, and, in the years since the Second World War especially, might have had experience of running a parish. The 'curate' in 1933 was a canon. Indeed, the present charity scheme insists upon the employment of a retired clergyman. It was decided that it would be more appropriate to call him 'Chaplain'. This stressed the fact that the appointment was to what was in reality a private church.

As the organisation of the charities was now secure, internal events became of prime interest. The number of Gaudy Days had risen to seven. Both Trustees and brethren felt that this was too many, and it was agreed to reduce them to two only, but that each brother should be entitled to bring a guest, and that the food should be made rather more luxurious. In 1995, due to a benefaction, the number of gaudies is now three and they are pleasant social occasions where brethren, Trustees, wives (on occasion) and all who work for St Cross join together.

The life of the brethren was naturally an internal interest of supreme importance. One of the brothers had personal problems. 'The Master also called attention to the case of Brother Croft, who has a wife who is giving a good deal of trouble and who could not be controlled by her husband.' The Master was given a free hand to deal with the matter, and Mrs. Croft was wise enough to accept instructions from him. He also mentioned the case of Brother Humphreys who 'had absented himself from the Hospital without leave and was still not back'. The Trustees decided that the Master should now give seven days' warning (presumably to the air, as Humphreys was not present) and then take action. Daldy later reported that Humphreys had not returned 'but that his sister had come to collect his belongings and it is assumed that he has resigned'. Thirty years later, the same phrase and assumption were used when Brother Collins married without obtaining the Trustees' permission, and then walked out with his new wife, leaving an empty flat behind him. The accounts also show expenditure of £8 18s. 0d. 'for an appliance for Brother Yates and a

42 *Two brothers of the present day—Brother Ashby of the Beaufort (Red) Foundation, and Brother Lister of the Hospital (Black) Foundation. Note the round badge with cardinal's hat and cross potent of the Red Brother and the cross potent alone of the Black Brother.*

contribution towards dentures for Brother Levett'. One of the brothers who died in 1932 was Brother Williams, who had been born in Lucknow during its siege in the Indian Mutiny. His father had been a clerk in Sago's garrison there. It is often astonishing how far back into what seems to be remote historical events the lives of brethren stretch.

Terminology came up again with the brothers. Some ex-servicemen from the First World War stuck to the ranks they had earned then. Once more, the Brothers' Council pointed out that there was only one title in St Cross, and that was 'Brother'. The same comment was to be made in the years after 1945, such is the reasonable pride in the name of 'Brother' in these charities.

For much of his Mastership, the Ven. Daldy was absent from St Cross, carrying out his duties as Archdeacon of Winchester. Consequently, a large portion of the work of Master fell on Canon Wainwright, the then Chaplain. In recognition of this fact, the Trustees permitted Wainwright to wear the cross of St Cross, a privilege normally reserved for the Master alone. They were careful to point out that this must in no way be regarded as creating a precedent.

In October 1935, the Ven. Dalby died. It was a sudden death, as the log book sadly records: 'The Master, Ven. Alfred E. Daldy, Archdeacon of Winchester, passed away while at breakfast'. The somewhat abrupt manner in which the Bishop went about replacing him—simply having a notice pinned to the church door stating his intention to collate Rev. Charles Bostock on 9 February 1936—naturally rather annoyed the Trustees. Collation means to institute someone to a benefice, and the Trustees pointed out that the scheme under which they had to work nowhere mentioned a benefice of St Cross, and that St Faith was only included as an act of grace. They felt that at the very least they should have been notified in advance of the choice, and that really there ought to have been some measure of consultation. The Bishop accepted the comments, and promised that there would be advance notice and consultation in the future. Had they been asked, the Trustees would have warmly welcomed the choice of Rev. Bostock, who was a graduate of Selwyn, Cambridge, and had been vicar and rural dean in Bournemouth.

One of the early events in his Mastership was the celebration of the 800th anniversary of the de Blois Foundation in 1936. This was certainly about four years too late, but nevertheless was graced by a visit from Dr. Garbett, then Bishop of Winchester and later Archbishop of York. There was a service in the church, attended by all the local civil and ecclesiastic dignatories, followed by lunch in the Brethren's Hall. Two garden parties were held, with enough visitors to demand the simultaneous use of the quad between Hall and church and the Master's garden at each. Finally, at 8 p.m., the day ended with a service of thanksgiving in the church.

These were difficult days, nationally and internationally. When Edward VIII abdicated, the Master and brethren sent a message of sympathy to Queen Mary, the Queen Mother, and received a gracious reply. More worrying was the threat of war. In July 1938 the Trustees decided to make the kitchen by the Brethren's Hall into a gas-proof shelter. The coal cellar was to become a temporary lavatory. All brethren's rooms were to have dark blinds fitted, and each brother was issued with a small hand torch. Soon, however, Chamberlain's visit to Munich seemed to guarantee peace, so the Master was instructed to collect into a safe place the gas masks that had been issued.

War, contrary to all hopes, soon came. Before the actual declaration, the Air Raid Warden for the district, Colonel Davidson, had ordered that the bulbs were to be removed from any outside lamps in the Hospital grounds. Very soon after the outbreak of war, St Faith's School was taken over as a First Aid Post, with the children temporarily transferred to Stanmore. Three stirrup pumps, a large water carrier, six galvanised buckets, and six buckets for sand, were bought to extend the fire precautions. Lighting was wired into the roof space of the church, and water tanks placed on the top of the roofs, which were themselves criss-crossed with iron ladders. More ladders led down to the ground, and a fireman's hose was installed in the choir. Later, all the lead roofing was covered with 'cement pumice blocks' as a defence against incendiary bombs. Efforts were made to camouflage the whole array of buildings. Some of the land in The Park was ploughed up, other parts were requisitioned 'for military purposes'. A machine-gun post was sited near 'the stables and yard'. The loft over the stable in the outer yard became an emergency food supply depot. The iron gates and railings were scheduled for requisition. All in all, peaceful St Cross took on a warlike stance.

In the midst of all this activity, the Master fell ill, and was forced to resign in December 1942. Unhappily, he did not enjoy his retirement for long, as he died in January 1943. Remembering the comments made at the last appointment, the Bishop of Winchester asked the Trustees if they had any names to put forward. They 'named a certain clergyman', and the Rev. Oswald Hunt, who had been a vicar and rural dean in Dorking, was appointed.

When the war ended, the Trustees discovered that one out-pensioner, Mr. Hindle, had not been paid since July 1940, as he lived in Jersey and had been under Nazi rule. He was now shown to be very much alive, so he was paid, as was clearly his due, his back pay amounting to £130—which was more than the basic annual pay for many workers at that time. He must have felt temporarily a wealthy man.

Rev. Hunt found that there were some brothers who caused difficulties amongst their fellows. There was no clause in the scheme allowing for the exclusion of such people, but now the Trustees decided that any brother who 'exerted a harmful influence among the other Brethren' should be dismissed. The Master also asked for discretion to vary the number of brothers, so that it did not always have to be up to 18 of the Hospital Foundation and up to 9 of the Noble Poverty Foundation. The new Welfare State, based on Beveridge's ideas, had removed the hardship of real poverty from some groups of people, and it would be useful to be able to appoint solely according to need and with no other criterion. The Charity Commissioners would not permit this, as in their eyes there were two separate charities, with two separate sets of funds and two separate conditions for entry. However, it was accepted that the stipends given to brothers should be linked to the terms of state aid, and that the amount given by St Cross could be reduced if it meant that the state would give more.

For centuries, brothers and parishioners alike had heard the services and sermons in the church without any artificial aids. Now it was felt that the acoustics were not 100 per cent, and amplifiers and speakers were installed in December 1947. They have been extended and improved twice since then.

Externally, too, the church needed some repair. Several bits of stone foliage as finials to the dripstones over the west door, were showing signs of wear. When Mr. Newman, the mason, saw them, he decided that they were virtually beyond repair and replaced them with grotesques of his own design. The architect was angry that this had happened, but the Trustees pointed out that it was merely the continuation of an old practice. As a matter of fact, in the east wall of the north transept there was a stone portrait of the mason involved in the 12th century, whilst the west wall had two stone portraits of his helpers. The grotesques remained.

One brother who had helped in the parish, Brother Kirchevall, died in 1949. He had played the organ with great success, had helped with the Sunday School, been 'an outstandingly efficient exhibitor' (or guide) and had trained other brethren in the duties. An Old Wykehamist and member of the Archaeological Society, he was much loved.

As St Cross was a charity, it was felt that using the homes provided as a base for a business was not allowed. Brother Radford was told that he could not call his quarters 'The Rosary' and advertise himself as a rose expert. He had apparently made 30 guineas from such expertise, and there was some feeling that perhaps this money should go to the

Charity. Eventually, he was allowed to keep his earnings. Brother Colson did some writing, but it was thought that his *Record of White's Club* was unlikely to gain sufficient royalties to make any action necessary. The feelings aroused by these discussions led to a new scheme (one of very many) being produced by the Charity Commissioners, which forbade the use of the Hospital for gain by the brethren. Twenty years later, Brother Young died, leaving an estate of £58,227. Several Trustees felt that someone with such means should never have been accepted and it was agreed that men with capital to that extent were not true cases for admission to either foundation.

A number of important documents were stored in St Cross, but had been both neglected and unsorted. In 1952, Barbara Carpenter Turner, Winchester's foremost local historian, commenced the work of sorting and saving the documents. She was later appointed Honorary Archivist, a post she held until 1993, and did much excellent and important work. Indeed, it is probable that most of the documents would have perished without her devotion. There were times when there was difficulty over access to these records, and it was decided by the Trustees that in future the Honorary Archivist for the time should attend every quarterly meeting and give a report on the Archives.

In 1953, the Rev. Oswald Hunt retired, and the Rev. Geoffrey Carlisle took over as Master. It is perhaps a sign of how the economic situation of the country had improved, that he at once began to talk of the difficulty in getting brothers, despite widespread advertising. This compares, for instance, with 1898 when there were 71 applicants for two vacancies to live in and 123 applying for three out-lier pensions.

A difficulty arose in connection with those who lived in. So many of the brothers over the years had been married, that occasional problems resulted over the position of their widows, if the husbands died whilst still at St Cross. Theoretically, they had no right to continue to live in their husband's flat, and should leave at once. The Trustees decided that in future widows should be allowed up to six months in which to find alternative accommodation.

Apart from themselves creating a link to the past, occasionally one or other of the brethren would deliberately look into history. During the Protectorate, the statue of the Virgin Mary, standing on the first pillar in the north aisle, had been pulled down. For 300 years, the base upon which it had stood remained unoccupied. Now, in 1960, Brother Danson gave a stone cross potent, as used in St Cross's arms, to replace the Virgin. It is this cross upon which the sun first shines on Holy Cross Day.

The church proved to be a considerable draw for film makers and television programme producers. In 1969, a film was made in the nave, involving 17 horses and one donkey. It must have been an interesting sight; however 'a rubber corrugated mat had been put down so that there was very little clearance required afterwards'. Strangely, Trollope's Barchester novels, based as they are on St Cross, were actually filmed elsewhere.

A measure of the success of the Charity Commissioners' oft amended schemes for St Cross, and of the work of the Master at this time, is that there was little or no exciting material in the minutes. Hence, when Rev. Carlisle resigned in 1970, it can only be said that he left an institution in good heart. Canon Felstead, the next Master, had been vicar of St Michael's, Southampton for the previous 25 years, and rural dean for the last 12 of them. One of his earliest acts was to accept the resignation of Isidore Harvey, who had been organist for 34 years and sub-organist at the Cathedral, and to appoint David Waldin in his place. Mr. Waldin still in 1995, although no longer organist in charge of the music, gives occasional valuable help with the music of the church. He was followed in the post by Clement McWilliam, whilst the present incumbent is Derek Beck. Clement is now a brother of St Cross, and so is able also to offer musical help on occasion. Music is still high on the list of priorities and excellence at St Cross.

What seems from all available records to be unique for the Hospital was the occasion when Brother Warner in 1975 followed in his father's footsteps as a member of the Hospital Foundation. What was even more remarkable, he actually took over the same rooms that his father had occupied, although, unlike his father, his wife was alive to share in the accommodation.

Brothers now had more freedom of action than ever before. They were asked in 1976 to wear their gowns and hats when going into the city, but many exercised their freedom not to do so. Brethren of previous ages had been told that it was their duty to be properly gowned and hatted, and had been taken to task if they failed to follow the rules. Later, mayors of the city were to request brethren to go dressed in their uniform into the city as it added to the dignity and interest of the city itself. Many brethren, however, did not wish to become a tourist attraction! To give them yet more time and freedom, in 1979, it was agreed that parishioners of St Faith's should be allowed to act as voluntary exhibitors, although generally there are still brothers who like to do this particular task.

Finance caused the Trustees a great deal of trouble. The inflation of the 1970s meant that the normal income was simply not enough to meet all demands. Consequently, with some misgivings, the Trustees decided to end the policy of providing pensions for people living out of the Hospital, the last one being paid in 1990. They also, even more reluctantly, found it necessary to charge the brethren for heating. Nowadays, brethren also pay something towards the rent of their flats, as is the custom in most other charities. There is a means test and every effort is made to ensure that all benefits from the state are obtained by anyone so entitled, and that the burden of any charge made by the Hospital is kept as low as possible.

In 1979, Canon Deedes became Master in succession to Canon Felstead. Canon Deedes had been for a short time a Royal Marines Officer, but his real career lay in the Church. His previous ministry had been for seven years as Team Minister for the city centre parish in Bournemouth, and he, like Felstead before him, had been rural dean. There was no connection between his installation and the fact that new amplifiers and microphones were installed in the church at the same time!

Once more, the scheme for St Cross was altered. There had been difficulty in filling vacancies for some years. Pension schemes throughout Britain were somewhat better than they had ever been in earlier times. Living in a community such as St Cross did not appeal to quite as many men as had formerly been the case. In 1984, the scheme was changed to allow men to be recruited to either foundation without reference to the particular qualifications of the applicant. Thus, men who might have previously been kept out because there were, say, only vacancies in the Red (or Noble Poverty) Brothers, and they did not qualify in that respect, could now come in. It was also agreed that, in future, all brothers-to-be should be interviewed jointly by the Master and one Trustee. Finally, the

Parochial Church Council should be allowed to elect one representative Trustee, who would cease to be a Trustee if he or she were no longer a member of the P.C.C.

In 1986, St Cross celebrated its 850th anniversary. To create a link with a 17th-century Master, Compton, a garden of American plants and trees was established. He became Bishop of London, and America was in his diocese. A small pageant of the history of St Cross was performed in the church. The real high mark, however, was the visit of Queen Elizabeth, the Queen Mother, on 8 July 1986. She received the Wayfarers' Dole from the Porter, Jim Heavens, and was taken round the establishment by the Master. As always, wherever she goes, she showed a keen and informed interest in St Cross.

A link with the past which ended in 1990 was when an order of the Charity Commission made the rector of Compton no longer an ex-officio Trustee. The other ex-officio Trustees put in place after the Chancery case remained as officers.

Customs continue to be observed, even though some of them have rather shorter histories than is thought. Senior Brother Murphy has custody of the silver mounted cane which is the symbol of his office. It was presented to the Hospital in January 1886 by Mr. and Mrs. Morris in order to help the senior man in the building. The Morrises also gave a 'rug, to be used by the brethren when drawn out in a chair'. Every week, the latest-gowned brother rings a hand-bell to summon the brethren to the Hall for 'Pay Parade'. Each brother is given a pound, which is traditionally tossed across the table to them. This has some whisper of the penny a day given across King Stephen's table to the workmen at the time of the early building works. However, in its present form it derives from the changing of food rations to a money payment in 1901. Previously, the bell had been used solely to summon the brothers to meals. Brother Lister leads the Master to his stall, bearing a staff on his shoulder. This is meant to represent the civil as opposed to ecclesiastic authority of the Master over the brethren. It is hard to pin down its origins, but it appears to have developed under North in about 1810. The cross carried by the Crucifer, Brother Kay, is again of 19th-century origin. However, there is evidence that a cross was carried before the Master or officiating clergy from very early times, as would have been quite normal.

Canon Deedes and his family built up an active and thriving parish, with many links to the brethren. Unfortunately, he suffered two heart attacks, but underwent successful heart by-pass surgery—so successful, indeed, that he was able to continue with his highly effective and active ministry. In 1992, he retired, leaving behind him much respect and affection.

The appointment of Canon Deedes had been made as a result of consultation with the Churchwardens, but without any input from the Trustees. This method, although it produced an excellent result, was felt by the Trustees to be, to say the least, unfortunate. The Acting Chairman, Mrs. Thackeray, wrote to the Bishop stating that as the Trustees owned the property, paid for all its maintenance, and were responsible under the scheme for all within it, they really were entitled to have their views sought. The Bishop agreed and the Scheme was altered by paragraph 26 which provided for consultation. When Canon Deedes retired, a joint committee of Trustees and the Churchwardens met to learn the Bishop's mind and to discuss his suggestion. The choice of Rev. Tony Outhwaite to be Master was heartily welcomed by this committee. Rev. Outhwaite had for a short while been an R.A.F. officer, but, like Colin Deedes, left the forces for the Church. He had been rector of New Milton for 21 years and rural dean of Christchurch, before taking up his appointment at St Cross in 1993. He has already shown skills of management, and a deep love of St Cross, its brethren and its institutions. One of his building changes has been to remove the oak partition in the vestry and to open the area to something like its old Norman or Anglo-Saxon appearance. Another building programme in hand is the conversion of the Hundred Menne's Hall into a Visitors' Centre.

In December, 1994, Rev. Ray Phillips was licensed as Chaplain to St Cross actually in the church. This is in itself unusual, as the licensing is almost always a private ceremony between Bishop and the priest concerned. There was some very real searching amongst old documents to discover whether there was a particular form of service which had to be followed. Rev. Phillips had followed a busy career overseas in Africa and the West Indies, before returning to England to take over Hillingdon parish, becoming rural dean. Perhaps even more noteworthy is the fact that as a boy he lived in Clausentum Road, attended St Faith's

43   *The present Master, Rev. A.S. Outhwaite. Photograph by kind permission of the* Hampshire Chronicle.

School, and was actually baptised in St Cross. His coming to work in the Hospital is a very real return to his roots.

From the time of the Chancery case, the Trustees have relied upon the advice of experts beyond the walls of the Hospital. Since 1974, John Clifton, as Clerk to the Trustees, has admirably advised on the law and kept the minutes of all meetings. As Receiver, Martin Lowry, aided by Mark Griffith, has been a staunch supporter in all matters to do with property and finance. However, it was recognised that it would be beneficial to have one administrator, filling the rôle of the old-time Steward, working within the Hospital, though not living in it. With that end in view, Mrs. Miriam Phillips was appointed Secretary to the Hospital in 1994, and works in what is the Trustees' room, where Rev. Andrewes had his drawing room when Master. She is on hand to provide the service formerly rendered by two officers working from offices in Winchester. There is thus an immediate point of contact for the brethren and any other person involved with the Hospital. It is a tremendous compliment to Mrs. Phillips' ability and enthusiasm that she fills the double gap completely. Additionally, the Hospital has its own architect, Michael Carden, who spends much time ensuring that the buildings remain in a good state. Much of the regular maintenance work is splendidly carried out by Mr. Emery, who succeeded

44   *St Cross from the air.*

two generations of the Newman family as the maintenance engineer. At the gate, Mr. Dowsett is a capable and enthusiastic first point of contact for all visitors.

Equal reliance is placed upon the willing help given by brothers. Brother Hodges has for seven years been an efficient verger. Brother Holmes, coming to St Cross after serving as Custos at the Cathedral, splendidly fills the rôle of sacristan. Brothers Dalgetty, Hatton and Stacey give able and willing help with services. Whenever asked, the brothers respond to help the church, just as parishioners are anxious to help the brothers.

The once proud acres owned by the Hospital, and the tithes due to it, have shrunk considerably. Its empire now consists, within St Cross, of property in St Cross Road, and Back Street, St Cross Dairy, Darts yard and the park land surrounding the Hospital itself. In addition it owns the Thatched Granary, paddock, cricket field, a 'Plantation', farmland and allotments at Whitchurch. It has, therefore, to rely heavily on the proceeds of investments. The Trustees can, of course, call on expert financial advice. St Cross, though finding life difficult, is now confidently looking forward to its next 860 years.

Appendix A

Brothers, as at January 1995

	Date Admitted
Brother Murphy (Senior Brother)	12 July 1976
Brother Dalgetty	10 April 1978
Brother Watkins	12 October 1981
Brother Kay	11 January 1982
Brother Wagner	16 March 1983
Brother Stacey	30 November 1984
Brother Francis	25 August 1986
Brother Holmes	12 September 1986
Brother Leonard	1 August 1987
Brother Payne	3 November 1987
Brother Hodges	4 March 1988
Brother Lister	31 May 1988
Brother Baker	1 August 1988
Brother Hatton	10 August 1990
Brother Lowe	15 February 1991
Brother O'Dell	1 December 1991
Brother Heavens	1 January 1992
Brother Ashby	1 August 1992
Brother Cadwallader	1 September 1992
Brother Grier	1 July 1993
Brother McWilliam	1 December 1993

APPENDIX C

Staff, as at January 1995

Secretary to the Hospital	Mrs. M. Phillips
Master's Secretary	Mrs. S. Wright
Porter	Mr. A. Dowsett
Matron	Mrs. R. Roots
Cook	Mrs. S. Butlin
Maintenance Engineer	Mr. C.T. Emery
Gardener	Miss K. Askew
Cleaner	Mr. I. Parker
Relief Matron	Mrs. M. Tiller
Relief Porter	Mr. P. Puddle

APPENDIX D

Masters of St Cross and Bishops of Winchester

Masters		Bishops of Winchester	
*c.*1132	Robert of Limesia	1129	Henry de Blois
*c.*1171	William —	1173	Richard of Ilchester
1185	Robert —	1189	Godfrey de Lucy
1204	Alan de Stoke	1205	Peter des Roches
*c.*1235	Humfrey de Myles	1239	William Ralegh
1241	Henry de Secusia		
1248	Geoffrey de Feringhes	1250	Aymer de Valance
*c.*1260	Thomas de Colchester	1261	William de Taunton
*c.*1268	Stephen de Wotton	1268	Nicholas of Ely
1289	Peter de Sancta Maria	1282	John Pontissara
1296	William de Wendlyng		
1299	Robert Maidstone	1305	Henry Woodlock
		1316	John de Sandale
		1319	Rigaud de Asserio
1321	Geoffrey de Welleford		
1322	Bertrand Asserio	1323	John de Stratford
1332	Peter de Galiciano	1333	Adam de Orleton
1335	William Edington		
1345	Raymund de Pelegrini	1345	William Edington
1346	Walter de Wetgang		
1346	Richard de Lutteshall		
1346	John Edington		
1348	William de Farlee		
1349	John Edington (re-collated)		
1366	William de Stowell	1366	William Wykeham
1368	Richard de Lyntesford		
1370	Roger de Cloune		
1374	Nicholas Wykeham		
1383	John de Campeden	1404	Cardinal Beaufort

Masters	**Bishops of Winchester**

Masters		Bishops of Winchester	
1410	John Forest		
1425	Thomas Forest	1447	William Waynflete
1463	Thomas Chaundler S.T.P.		
1465	William Westbury S.T.B.		
1473	Richard Harward LL.D.	1487	Peter Courtenay
1489	John Lychefield LL.D.		
1492	Robert Sherborne	1493	Thomas Langton
		1501	Richard Fox
1508	John Claymund		
1524	John Innocent LL.D.	1529	Cardinal Wolsey
		1531	Stephen Gardiner
		1551	John Poynet
1545	William Meadow M.A.	1553	Stephen Gardiner
		1556	John White
1557	John Leffe LL.D		
1557	Robert Raynolds LL.D		
1559	John Watson M.D.	1560	John Pilkington
		1561	Robert Horne
		1580	John Watson
1583	Robert Bennett S.T.P.	1584	Thomas Cooper
		1595	William Wickham
		1596	William Day
		1597	Thomas Bilson
1603	Arthur Lake S.T.B.		
1616	Sir Peter Young	1616	James Montagu
		1619	Lancelot Andrewes
1627	William Lewis S.T.P.	1628	Richard Neile
		1632	Walter Curle
1649	John Lisle		
1657	John Cooke		
1660	Richard Shute		
1660	William Lewis S.T.P. (re-instated)	1660	Brian Duppa
		1662	George Morley
1667	Henry Compton D.D.		
1675	William Harrison D.D.	1684	Peter Mews
1694	Abraham Markland D.D.	1707	Sir John Trelawny
		1721	Charles Trimnel
		1723	Richard Willis
1728	John Lynch D.D.	1734	Benjamin Hoadly
1760	John Hoadly LL.D.	1761	John Thomas
1776	Beilby Porteus D.D.	1781	Brownlow North
1788	John Lockman D.D.		

continued overleaf ...

Masters		**Bishops of Winchester**	
1808	Francis North M.A.	1820	George Tomline
		1827	Charles Sumner
1855	Lewis Humbert M.A.		
1868	William Andrewes M.A.	1869	Samuel Wilberforce
		1873	Edward Browne
		1893	Randall Davidson
1901	Hon. Alan Brodrick M.A.	1903	Edward Ryle
1909	Francis Causton M.A.	1911	Edward Talbot
		1924	Frank Woods
1928	Alfred Daldy M.A.	1932	Cyril Garbett
1936	Charles Bostock M.A.	1942	Mervyn Haigh
1943	Oswald Hunt M.A.		
1953	Geoffrey Carlisle M.A.	1953	Alwyn Williams
		1962	Falkner Allison
1970	Kenneth Felstead M.Sc.	1975	John Taylor
1980	Colin Deedes B.A.	1985	Colin James
1992	Anthony Outhwaite B.Sc.		

The Glass at Saint Cross

Much of the glass in the church is Victorian, the gifts of local families. A great deal of the west end windows was glazed as a result of money given by the Lowth family, and was made by Wailes. A 20th-century descendant of the donor was moved to comment that it was not a very good example of its genre. However, it is full of colour and the west Jesse window is impressive. The north-west aisle has two windows by Easton, commemorating the Hanburys, and dating from the between-the-wars period. Typically, they both have Easton's signature, in the form of a weather vane formed by the letters of his name. Again, many of the north transept windows were glassed by the Lowth family in the Victorian era. There is also a window in memory of Rev. Hon. Alan Broderick, which has the signs of Our Lord's passion in a shield, after the style of the great earlier Master, de Campeden. The most southerly of the eastern windows in the transept has some interesting glass in it. Clearly, it was originally a representation of the Trinity. What is left now is the top and bottom. At the top is the head of the Father, fitting on to his waist, with hands alongside on the arms of his golden throne. Central, and rising from an orb, is the stem of a crucifix, with Jesus' legs visible, but none of the rest of his body; the dove that would have hovered over the Father's chest has disappeared, together with the chest itself and the remainder of Our Lord's body on the crucifix. Below is a label with the wording 'Personis Trinis, miserere mei, Deus unus'. The normal order would be to reverse the last two phrases, and it could well be that the artist copied them down wrongly on to his glass. A large roundel holds a vase with five lilies springing from it, and another label marked 'Ave Maria'. A small head with halo fills up one corner. A similar but complete Trinity is to be found in the College. This glass is certainly no later than 1480, and may well be some twenty years prior to that. The Peace Chapel has some good examples of early 20th-century stained glass, including the 'Fortitude' window given by Mrs. Morris. The east window, above the altar, is a mix of ancient and modern. The modern consists of the four oblong windows containing the initials V.R., A.P., C.W., L.M.H. as requested in the gift of 'Z.O.'. The top two windows are St Swithun (to the north) and St Katharine (to the south). Each is identified by being named in the glass. These are slightly later than the Trinity window, and probably date from about 1490. The lower two windows are of the Virgin Mary and St John. They look upwards and inwards and are almost certainly part of a larger crucifixion window. From the colours used and the style, these two windows would seem to date from about 1480. High up in the first window in the clerestory of the south transept is the figure of St Gregory, with tiara and halo, superimposed on what could be called a simplified St John's cross. It is equally of the last quarter of the 15th century.

Just above the door at the top of the steps into the Brethren's Hall are fragments of glass dating from about 1200, which may well have been part of the original glazing in the church. They represent portions of stems, with yellow, white, green and red leaves. By comparison with similar work in Canterbury Cathedral and the Long Gallery of Winchester Cathedral's Deanery, it is deduced that this glass was the work of Frenchmen painting in England. Le Couteur gives it the accolade of saying that it is 'better in workmanship' than the Cathedral's. There are also 14th- and 15th-century fragments, including one piece representing a claw hammer with stained handle which was probably part of a larger passion scene. A 16th-century fragment depicts the arms of England and France quartered and surrounded by the Garter. Inside the halls, the windows show the arms of the royal family and those of Beaufort, differenced by the bordure and cardinal's hat. One of the windows in the passage down to the kitchen has the motto of Sherborne plus the date 1497, with the four and seven in the old script. There is also in this window a portcullis, Henry VII's favourite badge.

In the Master's Office is a glass which unites de Blois with Compton. Alongside it is a glass with the arms of Speaker Cornwall. In the staircase up to the Hospital Secretary's office, there is a window stained with R.T.S., for Sherborne. A 16th-century Flemish roundel depicts the nativity, whilst a second of the same period and workmanship shows Jesus' presentation at the Temple.

Inside the Secretary's office are a number of widows bearing arms—Fox, Gardiner, Wickham, the city of Winchester, Dean Mason, the royal arms. This last has I.R. for James Rex, the French and British arms and the date 1623. The rest date from the 16th century but are generally regarded as of inferior workmanship, with the exception of that of Sir John Mason. The 17th-century version of the arms of Oxford University, dated 1623, appear in one window. There is also an early 16th-century Flemish roundel of Christ's trial, a similarly dated glass which seems at one time to have been a pierced heart, hands, feet and cross, and 17th-century glass of Mary mourning over the body of Jesus.

Bibliography

Principally, the archives of St Cross, now in the Hampshire Records Office

Baigent, Frederick, 'On the Church of the Hospital of the Holy Cross.' Written notes in British Library (1860)

Bailey, Brian, *Almshouses* (1988)

Biddle, Martin (ed.) *Winchester Studies* (1990)

Bogan, Peter, *The Burial Ground of St James*, (unpublished, Winchester)

Carpenter Turner, Barbara, *History of Hampshire* (1978)

Carpenter Turner, Barbara, *History of Winchester* (1992)

Chapman, R.W. (ed.), *Letters of Samuel Johnson* (1952)

Clay, Rotha, *The Medieval Hospitals of England* (1911)

Defoe, Daniel, *A Journey through England* (1723)

Duthy, John, *Sketches of Hampshire* (1839)

English Law, Reports for, 1853-1857

Godwin, *De Praesulibus* (1223)

Goodman, Arthur, *Chartulary of Winchester Cathedral* (1927)

Humbert, Lewis, *The Hospital of St Cross and the Almshouse of Noble Poverty* (1898)

Kusaba, Yosio, *Architectural History of the Church of St Cross* (1983)

Leach, Arthur, *The Schools of Medieval England* (1915)

Mee, Arthur, *Hampshire* (1949)

Milner, John, *History of Winchester* (1798)

Pevsner, Nicholas, *Buildings of Hampshire* (1979)

Thorn, William, *St Cross Hospital* (1899)

The Victoria County History of Hampshire, especially Vol. II, pp. 193-197 (1903)

Woodward, B.B., *History of Winchester* (1834)

Other Sources

Carden, Michael, *Talks and walks around the Church, re: architecture and stages of building*

Bro. Heavens, Jim, *Talks and walks around the Church*

Bro. Holmes, Roy, *Talks and walks around the Church*

Index